CISTERCIAN FATHERS SERIES: NUMBER THIRTY-SIX

STEPHEN OF SAWLEY

TREATISES

CISTERCIAN FATHERS SERIES: NUMBER THIRTY-SIX

STEPHEN OF SAWLEY

TREATISES

Translated by JEREMIAH F. O'SULLIVAN

Edited for publication by
BEDE K. LACKNER

Cistercian Publications Inc.
Kalamazoo, Michigan
1984

Stephen of Sawley (Stephen of Easton) †1252.

The translations have been made from the following editions:

André Wilmart. 'Les méditations d'Étienne de Sallai sur les joies de la Vierge Marie', *Revue d'ascétique et de mystique,* 10 (1929) 268-415.

André Wilmart. 'Le triple exercice d'Étienne de Sallai', *Revue d'ascétique et de mystique,* 11 (1930) 355-374.

Edmund Mikkers. 'Un *Speculum novitii* inédit d'Étienne de Salley', *Collectanea OCR,* 8 (1946) 17-68.

Edmond Mikkers. 'Un traité inédit d'Étienne de Salley sur la psalmodie', *Cîteaux,* 23 (1972) 245-288.

Available from the publisher
Cistercian Publications Inc.
WMU Station   Kalamazoo, Michigan 49008

Available in Britain and Europe from
A. R. Mowbray & Co Ltd   St Thomas House
Becket Street   Oxford OX1 1SJ

The work of Cistercian Publications is made possible in part by support from Western Michigan University.

Typeset by Gale Akins, Kalamazoo
Printed in the United States of America

Library of Congress Cataloguing in Publication Data:
Stephen, of Sawley, d. 1272.
    Treatises.

    (Cistercian Fathers series ; no. 36)
    Bibliography: p. 191
    Includes index.
    1. Monastic and religious life—Early works to 1800.
2. Cistercians—Spiritual life—Early works to 1800.
I. Lackner, Bede K.   II. Title.   III. Series.
BX2435.S732513 1984   248.4'820942   83-15249
ISBN 0-87907-636-4

To Claire

TABLE OF CONTENTS

PREFACE

THIS VOLUME was prepared by Jeremiah Francis O'Sullivan, a great scholar and amazing Irishman. Always fascinated with medieval monasticism, especially in its Cistercian expression, he spent a lifetime exploring this most rewarding subject. He generously shared the insights of his ever-active mind with his students at Fordham University and, in the process, trained a whole generation of Cistercian scholars who are anxious to continue where he left off.

During his long years of teaching, Jeremiah O'Sullivan managed to find the time, in spite of his many responsibilities, to work on his favorite scholarly projects. Thus when he retired in 1968, he had completed several book-length manuscripts, combining the fruits of his vast erudition with uniquely personal observations. Many of these manuscripts are now being readied for publication.

While pursuing his own projects, Jeremiah O'Sullivan also became an enthusiastic sponsor and supporter of Cistercian Publications, accepting several challenging commissions from the nascent firm. He volunteered to translate 'difficult' medieval cistercian classics; this became for him a labor of love in spite of the inroads made by a treacherous illness which eventually felled him in 1974.

One of his last undertakings was devoted to the writings of Stephen of Sawley, a little known cistercian author of the thirteenth century. Able to complete the rough and heavy work and endow it with scholarly notes, he had no time for the finishing touches. These were to be made by a disciple, who assumed his task with both reverence and humility. Given the differences in temperaments and literary styles of the two collaborators, the final product may well display a certain diversity. But while this is regrettable, it will not diminish the substance of the work.

In his scholarly labors Jeremiah O'Sullivan enjoyed the devoted assistance of his wife Claire. She typed the many thousand pages of his manuscripts with a competence which even experts find pleasant to behold. And she encouraged and supported the students of her late husband with a truly generous heart. It is, therefore, a joy to dedicate this volume to Claire O'Sullivan.

B. K. L.

INTRODUCTION

S TEPHEN OF SAWLEY, who successively headed three English Cistercian abbeys during the first half of the thirteenth century, is mentioned in a number of contemporary documents. Some twenty dated documents between the years 1225 and 1251 list his name, and there are at least as many references in undated records. All these references, occasioned by transactions of an economic nature, have been known for some time and were printed in various source collections during the nineteenth century.

Less known is the fact that Stephen also composed a number of treatises on the spiritual life; thus Charles de Visch did not list him in his *Bibliographia Scriptorum Sacri Ordinis Cisterciensis,* published in 1649. But three centuries later, Léopold Delisle discovered one of these works which a near-contemporary rubric explicitly attributed to Stephen of Sawley. It was edited by André Wilmart only in 1929, under the title of *Les méditations d'Étienne de Sallai sur les joies de la Sainte Vierge* (Meditations on the Joys of the Holy Virgin Mary).[1] One year later (1930) Wilmart published another treatise, which he called *Le triple exercice d'Etienne de Sallai* (The Threefold Exercise of Stephen of Sallay) and argued from textual agreements between this work and the *Meditations* that it, too, has been authored by Stephen of Sawley.[2] Then, in 1946, Edmond Mikkers, OCSO, published 'Un *Speculum Novitii* inédit *d'Etienne de Sallay'*, claiming it as still another of Stephen's writings on the basis of strong internal evidence and a corrected reference which would list Stephen of Sawley, rather than Stephen of Savigny, as the work's author.[3] Finally, in 1972, Mikkers also published a longer work entitled *De informatione mentis circa psalmo-*

diam diei ac noctis (On Preparing the Mind for the Divine Office) and proposed that it contained sufficient evidence to be ascribed to Stephen of Sawley.[4] Taken together, the four works are quite comprehensive in nature: they offer practical advice to young Cistercians about the basic elements of the monastic life, above all the life of prayer.

Wilmart and Mikkers reconstructed Stephen's writings from a handful of extant manuscripts. They prefaced their editions with general introductory remarks, without offering an exhaustive analysis of the works themselves; nor has this been done to the present day. The translation of the four treatises and their publication by Cistercian Publications in a single volume will, we hope, inspire such a study in the not too distant future, especially once the question of authorship has been more firmly established.

But all this reveals rather little about Stephen himself. Indeed, Stephen of Sawley appears to us as an anonymous hero in the best medieval tradition. He said nothing about himself in his writings, and what his contemporaries have left by way of information is little more than mere statistical data. Hence there is no external evidence or detailed information about Stephen, his background, his personality, or even his activities.

This means that Stephen was to be known by his writings or from his writings. While a source of this kind may be woefully meager and inadequate, it still offers more objective —and thus, lasting—information than what a possible hearsay evidence of his contemporaries could possibly report. Also, the picture he drew about the daily life and the spiritual exercises of a typical thirteenth-century english monastery certainly mirrored Stephen's own life and his religious convictions.

In spite of the lack of information, we know from a mid-fifteenth-century reference that Stephen was born at Eston (Easton) in Yorkshire, toward the end of the twelfth century; hence he is also known as Stephen of Easton, after his

place of origin.[3] Because Easton had economic ties with the
Cistercian abbey of Fountains, it is hardly surprising that
upon receiving a call to the monastic life, Stephen entered
this great abbey as a novice. At Fountains he received his religious formation as called for by the Rule of St Benedict and
the cistercian usages which were observed, more or less uni-
formly, throughout the Order. Some time after 1215 he was
appointed cellarer of the monastery and charged with the
physical and material well-being of the community and the
supervision and spiritual guidance of the laybrothers. He ad-
ministered his office for a number of years. In 1223 the
monks of Sawley, not very far from Fountains, elected him as
their abbot—not an unusual event for the statutes of the
Order gave the white monks the right to elect their abbots
from the members of abbeys of their respective filiations.
Obviously, an awareness of Stephen's renown and of his
qualifications preceded his election.

As the fourth abbot of Sawley (Sallai, Salley) in the south
of Yorkshire, Stephen led his charges for ten years. The
dated charters which refer to Stephen's abbacy range from
24 January 1225, to 19 October 1233. During this period
Stephen also figured in the annals of the Cistercian General
Chapters. In 1226 he journeyed to Cîteaux, the mother-
house of all Cistercian abbeys, to attend the annual General
Chapter of the Order, which customarily met in the middle of
September. In one of its decisions Stephen was asked, with
two other abbots, to settle a controversy involving disputed
properties between the abbots of Fountains and Jervaulx,
through mediation or an imposed settlement. Stephen also
attended the next General Chapter in 1230, which asked him
to inform the abbots of Rievaulx and Clive of the condemnation of the abbot of Stanley, who had failed to prevent
a duel.

In 1234 Stephen was chosen abbot of Newminster in
Northumberland, the motherhouse of Sawley. While no
information is extant for the years 1234-1240, in a number

of charters drawn up between 1240–1247 he is mentioned as
abbot of Newminster. In 1240 the General Chapter gave
Stephen permission to attend its meetings at four-year
intervals rather than annually, with the proviso that this concession would not be granted to his successors. It was, therefore, a personal dispensation. It may have been given to
Stephen for reasons of health, but it could hardly have been a
concession to his advancing years, for in 1247 he was made
abbot of Fountains, the mother-house of Newminster and
one of the most illustrious houses of the Order, returning to
the place where he had begun his monastic life several decades
earlier.

Stephen governed the abbey for four years, six months
and five days, until his apparently sudden death on Friday,
8 September 1252, while visiting Vaudy, a daughter-house of
Fountains in Lincolnshire. The monks of Vaudy buried him
in their chapter room, in front of the abbot's chair. Documents drafted a few months later refer to him as *quondam
abbas*. Besides keeping his bodily remains, Vaudy also cultivated Stephen's memory, for according to its fifteenth-
century chronicler, the inscription over Stephen's burial site
included the words 'where [in heaven] he is radiant in glory
as a worker of miracles', clearly indicating that Stephen had
died in the odor of sanctity.

This is all the documents say about Stephen. They do not
mention whether he attended any school before entering the
monastery or whether he received any additional formation
beside his monastic training. In view of Stephen's dislike of
dialectics this seems rather unlikely. Yet Stephen was well-
versed in theology and philosophy—even in the art of
dialectics—and he had obvious literary talents. He also made
references to ancient history, the siege of Jerusalem by
Vespasian and Titus, and quoted from Horace's *Ars Poetica*,
a work which in all likelihood was not kept in Cistercian
armaria. As a general principle, Stephen insisted that learning
should not be sought for the sake of increasing one's

knowledge or being able to correct others, but for the sake of improving oneself.

Additional clues about Stephen's education may be gathered from his writings. They reveal an intimate knowledge of the Scriptures, the liturgy, and the Church Fathers. Some passages reveal a theological expertise which exceeded the knowledge of an amateur; they also show a standard philosophical terminology and an unmistakable predilection for the number three. Moreover, Stephen told his readers what they should read. Novices were instructed to study the Scriptures in depth, to read the Fathers, especially St Augustine and the standard monastic writings, such as the *Lives of the Desert Fathers,* the works of John Cassian, and the letters of St Jerome which deal with the monastic life. From the Cistercian world he singled out St Bernard, William of Saint Thierry, Aelred of Rievaulx, and Gilbert of Hoyland, as well as the liturgical books and the Customary of the Order. If he counseled the study of these authors or works, we may safely assume that he himself had read and was fully acquainted with them.

The same can be said about the works Stephen used or cited in his treatises. In addition to the sources just listed, he borrowed from Amadeus of Lausanne, certain psalm commentaries, and several popular treatises and legends.

While Stephen was not one of the great cistercian authors, he was nevertheless a gifted writer. He knew his grammar well and was able to construct long sentences without losing the thread of his narrative or argument. His style abounds in assonances, characteristic phrases, inversions, unusual expressions, proverbs, and aphorisms. He repeats favorite expressions but also uses synonyms. His style has a definite rhythm and considerable polish and a simple elegance, and his metrics show great perfection. In the use of his sources and literary borrowings, in the choice of his themes and in his composition he shows an amazing degree of independence and a lack of ambiguities, not least because he seeks to help, rather than merely please, his reader.

Unlike other cistercian authors, Stephen was chiefly concerned with the young and the beginners, anxious to teach them how to pray and, more generally, how to be good monks. As a practical man he gave a great deal of practical advice to his readers. He told novices to memorize portions of their *lectio* and apply the scriptural texts to their own situation. He voiced his belief that a very effective way to fight temptations is to make the sign of the cross or to join the community during work, and that the best method to fight insomnia is to pray the Seven Penitential Psalms or to recite the lengthy Athanasian Creed. His practical sense enabled him to propose small steps or even shortcuts whenever there was a lack of time. In like manner he insisted that one must not seek quick results in the spiritual life but proceed gradually in accordance with the promptings of grace.

The features of Stephen's personality may also be deduced from the nature of his various positions. The fact that Stephen held the office of cellarer and was elected abbot of three prestigious monasteries implies that he was not merely a good leader and administrator, but also an experienced director of souls, for the legislation of Cîteaux required such expertise from its prospective abbots. And since the Cistercian General Chapter enlisted him as a peacemaker, he must have been endowed with the necessary diplomatic skills to carry out his mission successfully. Finally, Stephen's participation in local transactions, where he often figured as a witness, suggests a certain prominence in his region.

Throughout his writings Stephen appears to us as a sincere and convinced religious, without hesitation about his religious convictions or the monastic way of life. To him the latter was a gift from God which must be accepted with gratitude and ever cultivated. In this the Rule of St Benedict, the Institutes of the Cistercian Order, and the good example of other monks served him as powerful aids. He would be faithful to his profession and never yield to the temptation that he could do better in another monastery.

Stephen also had an excellent knowledge of human nature, and was fully aware of his own limitations. He called himself repeatedly, 'a most untrustworthy sinner', and reminded his reader also about his shortcomings. Accordingly, whenever he set out to write he did not trust in himself but relied on the assistance of the saints, above all the Virgin Mary. With such a disposition he offered his words as words of instruction and counsel rather than as directives or commands, as some spiritual writers are wont to do.

Stephen knew that in consequence of the Fall, humankind entangled itself in an endless series of miseries involving both the body and the soul. The 'mirror' he drew up for novices as an aid in examining their consciences contains an amazingly specific list of human failings based on a certain knowledge of human psychology. This is also evident from his list of some twenty different temptations, originating in the mind, the body, and the emotions, which usually threaten a novice or a monk. He explored the causes and the circumstances of wrongdoings and distinguished between what is done intentionally or unintentionally, wittingly or unwittingly; he also knew that certain acts are committed only in the mind, and that sins should be confessed to the extent they are remembered then and there.

A careful reading of Stephen's writings does reveal a few personal references. Stephen was 'irritated' when requested to write and 'dissembled' and kept silent for some time. In the end he agreed to put in writing what he had learned from his own experience, because he was prodded to do so by a friend, at times addressed also as 'dear son'. He promised results if his advice were followed. When one of his writings turned out to be rather long, he concluded that he had become 'unwise' but added at once that this must be ascribed to the friend who had asked him to write in the first place. On one occasion Stephen revealed that a certain monk longed for the prolongation of Matins until daylight so that he could think more about Christ and the goodness of God. In another passage he mentioned that while he was writing his treatise on the psalmody one of the monks became so ecstatic during the recitation of Psalm 88,[6] thinking about the Infant of Bethlehem, that he could hardly retain control over his emotions. In both instances Stephen may have been revealing his own feelings, for he offered rather specific details about the experiences in question.

Not a 'professional' writer, Stephen expressed a reluctance to write that stemmed from his realization that spiritual topics are better meditated upon, or even spoken of, than written about. He knew that everyone has his own unique make-up and mode of action, that the more advanced have acquired a much greater experience and that, as a general rule, it is never safe to impose personal views on others, especially on the young. He believed that one must speak less rather than more about this subject matter, which cannot be sufficiently explained in human words. Here we may very well have a reference to mystical graces.

Any attempt to describe and evaluate the four treatises labors under certain handicaps. The authorship of three of the works has by no means been settled, nor is the date of the four sufficiently known. And as yet there is no critical edition available. Hence, it is not possible to draw conclusions from the four treatises as if they were an organic unit. One must treat the works individually. Since one of the four treatises is directly attributed to Stephen of Sawley, it seems logical to introduce this work first and then present the other writings in the order of their publication.

The treatise which André Wilmart published in 1929 is entitled *Meditations on the Joys of the Blessed Virgin Mary.* A late-medieval reference listed Stephen of Sawley as its author and stated that he wrote the work at the request of an unknown monk. The author tells us that he was reluctant at first to write because of the difficulties involved in a treatment of sublime subjects by mere human words, but eventually agreed to take up his pen for the benefit of the 'simple', a term referring to the novices, the young, the simple-witted, and those in the preliminary stages of the spiritual life. Accordingly, he composed fifteen meditations on the joys of the Virgin Mary, as they were felt by Mary herself, by the angels and saints in heaven and by men on earth, in order to enflame souls with the love of the Blessed Virgin. These *Meditations* are arranged in three groups of five meditations, with a *Pause* after the first and second quinary serving as a brief recapitulation to ensure a better retention of the preceding material.

The fifteen meditations are similarly constructed: a longer *Meditation* on the joys of Mary is followed by a brief summary or *Joy* addressed to the Blessed Virgin, and by a *Prayer* which asks for the grace corresponding to what is being meditated upon. The individual meditation is concluded by an expanded version of the *Hail Mary,* possibly as it was then used in Yorkshire, though Stephen merely called it 'the *Ave Maria,* supplemented by certain expressions of love'.

Stephen meditates on the joys of Mary in their chronological sequence: The first five meditations review Mary's joys from the time of her own birth to the birth of Christ; the second consider Mary's joys from the birth of Christ to his Passion; the third dwell on the joys Mary experienced between Christ's Passion and her own assumption into heaven.

The joys are always connected with significant events in the life of Christ. In Stephen's view, these events must be seen in their proper context, i.e., with all their details, circumstances, and implications, as if they were being perceived by an actual witness. Some of the joys were connected with Christ's greatest sufferings; when Mary saw her Son nailed to the Cross and exposed to all kinds of vilifications, she experienced also immense joys, conscious of man's imminent redemption.

The fifteen petitions alluding to her joys ask Mary in a number of ways to help man overcome his infirmities—of body, mind, and soul—to reject sin and the seductions of this transitory world and to labor, instead, for the everlasting rewards of heaven.

The *Meditations* are tender and affective considerations of the great moments of the life of Mary, the Mother of Jesus, which are also the great mysteries of the christian faith. Drawing from the Scriptures, especially the accounts of St Luke and St Matthew, the cistercian liturgy, and the great cistercian authors, Stephen offers a rich theological content: Mary is absolutely beautiful, in body and in soul, because she has received the fullness of grace and even God himself. Hence she is rightly called the Queen of Heaven, Empress of the Angels, the Mistress of the World. But, as the Mother of Christ, she guides the hands of her Son and is thus also the Mother of Mercy, the hope of the wretched and the reconciliation of sinners. Stephen strongly insists that all these prerogatives were God-given and not the fruit of human efforts. Mary was singled out by the Holy Trinity; God himself had chosen to dwell in her and wished to save mankind through her. One has then every reason to develop a strong and tender devotion to Mary, this uniquely powerful advocate.

Stephen used a definite method throughout this work; this is rather astonishing, for methodical prayer was thought to have originated only in the sixteenth century. The joys considered clearly prefigure the coming devotion of the Rosary. But, most importantly, Stephen's *Meditations* emphasize that all marian devotion must be scriptural and that such devotion is an essential part of the monk's spiritual life.

The second—anonymous—treatise published by Wilmart in 1930 is much shorter. Comparing it with Stephen's *Meditations,* Wilmart reached the conclusion that it too was his work. This he deduced from the similarity of the two prologues and a number of literary arguments. The work itself consists of three meditations; since it had no title, Wilmart called it *Triple Exercise* (Threefold Exercise). This work, too, had been written at the request of a monk. The author was again reluctant to write but he eventually gave in, realizing he could be helpful to the young and the simple in their spiritual life.

The purpose of the three meditations was therefore to establish a spiritual bond between God and the individual soul through methodical reflections offered by the author. Far from seeking to understand God through the intellect or to satisfy man's curiosity, they were meant to be vehicles of the faith. Accordingly, the meditations concentrate on God, the Virgin Mary, and the heavenly Jerusalem. The first two exercises are quite short, the third much longer, with an extensive treatment of the heavenly hosts.

The first meditation ponders God and his goodness toward man. God gave countless supernatural and natural gifts to man, whom He created in his own image and made the participant of his heavenly glory. Yet man failed and squandered his treasures and thus drew upon himself endless punishments and troubles in this valley of tears. But man is not left to himself: he can always return to a waiting God who overlooks his sins and is eager to save him. For this unceasing concern he owes total gratitude and love to the three Divine Persons who individually involve themselves in man's salvation.

The second meditation briefly summarizes what St Bernard had said in his sermons for the second Sunday within the octave of the Assumption. It reviews the God-given privileges of the Virgin Mary, especially her role as intercessor, mediatrix, and advocate, through which she reconciles man with her divine Son, making him a participant of her heavenly glory.

The third meditation considers the fulfillment of the divine plan of salvation in the heavenly city of Jerusalem, examining at length the joys and various ministrations of the angels and

saints so as to inspire man to seek their help in this life and
thus eventually join them in heaven.

The *Threefold Exercise,* which draws on the Bible, the
cistercian liturgy, and the writings of Augustine and Bernard,
is a very reassuring work. It stresses fallen man's chances,
given God's goodness and the assistance of powerful inter-
cessors in heaven. It may seem astonishing that between the
meditations on God and the heavenly Jerusalem we find a
meditation on Mary and not Christ. But, this was done on
purpose, for Mary is not a replacement of Christ, but a
re-producer of Christ. Her role is to make Jesus present and
to lead all to Jesus. Stephen's marian devotion is firmly
rooted in the Gospel and, therefore, truly 'evangelical'.

The third work to be considered, called *Speculum Novi-
tiorum,* or *Mirror for Novices,* was published by Edmund
Mikkers in 1946. It is even more practical than the treatises
already mentioned. It is a spiritual directory designed to
instruct and guide the Cistercian novice in the daily round of
monastic exercises, both in his devotional and prayer life and
the practice of the virtues and in the simple performance of
his manifold daily duties. Its value lies in the fact that neither
the Rule of St Benedict nor the cistercian authors treat this
subject at length or in a systematic fashion, so that cistercian
generations simply relied on accepted norms and traditions.

As Mikkers has pointed out, the *Mirror* shows numerous
similarities with the two works mentioned above; the same
style, the use of characteristic—at times uncommon—expressions, and the same manner of quoting, all of which speaks in
favor of Stephen's authorship. Moreover, some of the extant
manuscripts ascribe the work to Stephen of *Lexington* who,
in Mikkers' view, could not have been its author but could
have been mistaken by the copyist for Stephen of *Sawley.*
Finally, the *Mirror* has the same strong points as the other
two writings. It has the same preoccupation with mental
prayer, the same concern for simplicity, and the same
methodical approach. Some of the sources used by its author

are from Stephen of Sawley's time, a fact which should not be overlooked. Now that manuscripts older than the sixteenth-century text used by Mikkers have been found, however, additional information may well be forthcoming and lead to a better understanding of the work itself.

The *Mirror For Novices* is divided into twenty-four chapters. Half of these are devoted to the subject of prayer, while the remaining chapters impart practical spiritual guidance about the virtues and vices and the most important components of the daily schedule, as the monks' chapter, work, meals, and *lectio*. Its first chapter has a detailed examination of conscience, while the last chapter offers numerous practical suggestions on how to fight the temptations usually encountered by a novice. These two chapters are particularly revealing because they say a great deal about the inner life, i.e. the thought world and particular concerns of individual novices and also monks.

The chapters on prayer discuss in some detail the monks' choir, individual meditation, and private prayer, but they make only brief allusions to the offices of the Virgin Mary and of the Dead which were by then also said in cistercian houses. Stephen tells the novice how to prepare for prayer and what to do during prayer. And, as in the *Meditations,* he briefly recapitulates what he had already said. Stephen strongly suggests that during prayer the novice should above all think about the life and passion of Christ. He stresses the need to be grateful to God for his innumerable gifts to humankind. Reflecting on them, the novice will come to see things within the context of salvation history and thus feel obligated to pray not only for limited intentions but for the well-being and the salvation of the whole world.

To enlighten the novice, Stephen proposes seven different methods of meditation: admiration, praise, comparison, longing, trustfulness, rejoicing, and thanksgiving, each time listing appropriate scriptural passages to demonstrate his point. For a full prayer life he also insisted on the need to say private prayers. He wished that they be said twice each day. These prayers were not to stress personal inventiveness or rely on more or less suitable manuals but were to utilize authentic prayers, i.e., the psalms and hymns of the liturgy and certain collects.

To advance in the spiritual life, Stephen additionally urged the novice to attend private Masses gladly, to go to sacramental confession once every week, and to confess his external shortcomings in the chapter of faults. During chapter, when accusing himself or being proclaimed by others, he was not to look for excuses, but to follow the example of Christ who suffered many insults even though he was completely innocent, and thus to learn the true meaning of correction and the value of monastic discipline.

The author spoke in some detail about the *lectio divina*, an essential element of the monastic schedule. Stephen felt that it is best done at the third hour of the day. It should concentrate initially on the liturgical books of the Order, the lives of the saints, the 'more solid food' of the Old and New Testaments, the Church Fathers (Augustine), the monastic classics (John Cassian), and the cistercian authors. According to Stephen, God wishes that the Scriptures be not just known and remembered, but above all lived; for Scripture is like a mirror in which the soul can see itself in a true reflection and work on its improvement. On the other hand, Stephen condemned any dealing with books on dialectics, because sophistry in the sacred and profane subjects will disturb the peace and tranquility of the soul.

Among the virtues, Stephen stressed the importance of obedience. He believed that obedience assures eternal salvation and that every Cistercian monk would save his soul if he loved his Order, i.e., accepted a life of obedience under his abbot. Among the vices, boastfulness is singled out for condemnation, because everyone who publicizes his own good works is liable to fall victim to pride, even if this remains hidden from others. One should rather look for the good in others and be thankful for an example worthy of imitation.

The *Mirror For Novices* reveals a great deal about the spiritual life of thirteenth-century english cistercian monasteries and the interior life of their monks. It may serve as a companion to the *Usus Monachorum*[7] and explain several of its points. The work had an impact also on the outside world; Richard Rolle seems to have known it. In many ways it retains its usefulness in our own days.

In 1972 E. Mikkers published the fourth and last treatise that has been ascribed to Stephen of Sawley. Extant in a single manuscript from the thirteenth or fourteenth century, it is inscribed *De informatione mentis circa psalmodiam diei ac noctis,* i.e., an essay for those concerned about a fruitful recitation of the psalms during the divine office. St Benedict had prescribed in his Rule that his monks should recite the one hundred-fifty psalms in the course of one week. The Cistercians faithfully adhered to his injunctions. Since their office consisted largely of psalms and since the monks spent several hours each day reciting them in the chapel, a work of this kind had an obvious importance for the novice or the beginner.

The great cistercian authors explored every aspect of the spiritual life but did not produce an introductory work on the divine office. St Bernard made only occasional references to it. He stressed its usefulness, urged that it be recited wisely— i.e., involving the heart, as the letter without the spirit kills— and gently but firmly rebuked those who allowed themselves to be overcome by fatigue during it. Caesarius of Heisterbach recorded similar distractions and incidents during psalmody.

The request of a monk for help in fighting distractions induced Stephen of Sawley to compose his treatise on the psalmody. He felt uneasy about the project, claiming personal insufficiencies and the need to respect individual differences, and also the dangers that arise when personal

ways are imposed on others. When he proposed a few points
drawn from his own experience, he did not wish to do
violence to someone else's way or to deny the legitimacy and
validity of more refined expectations.

As in the case of the two previous works, there is no external evidence in support of Stephen of Sawley's authorship.
Internal evidence, however allows a number of conclusions:
the author was certainly a Cistercian monk, for he followed
the Cistercian psalm distribution, refered to the Cistercian
Book of Usages, insisted on observing the Order's legislation,
and quoted from several Cistercian authors. Also, the original
manuscript hails from the city of Durham, which is in the
vicinity of both Newminster and Fountains and, therefore,
quite possibly, from one of the two abbeys. Then there is the
author's expressed wish to write for the benefit of the simple
and the young, which was also given as the cause for writing
the other treatises. Finally, it shows the same concern for the
divine office as the other works; in fact, certain parts of the
treatise are simply expanded versions of topics discussed in
the other three works.

The treatise has a lengthy prologue, forty chapters, and a
rather short conclusion. The chapters themselves form three
clearly discernible units: Chapters 1-9 are introductory in
nature, dealing with the psalmody, the Lord's Prayer and the
Apostles' Creed in general terms. Chapters 10-32 list the
themes of the psalms as they are distributed in the Cistercian
office. The individual hours of the weekly office are treated
as follows: Matins (chs. 4-16), Lauds (chs. 17-23), Prime
(chs. 24-30), the Little Hours and Vespers (ch. 31) and
Compline (ch. 32). The third part, i.e., chapters 33-40, apply
a single theme—Christ's Passion—to the canonical hours of
the day.

Stephen seems to have used the *Glossa ordinaria* attributed
to Anselm of Laon, the commentary of Peter Lombard, and,
possibly, some works of St Augustine as well as Bede's
commentaries. His other sources included Scripture, the Rule

of St Benedict, the cistercian liturgy, and the writings of St Bernard and Aelred of Rievaulx.

According to the prologue, the author's aim was to show how to keep in check the mind's wanderings and to offer practical and concrete examples for the benefit of those who for one reason or another had been unable to consult the available commentaries. Stephen taught his reader how to pray the psalms, how to make the psalmody—i.e., the divine office—into a spiritual celebration and thus to contribute to the monk's spiritual growth. This goal called for a personal involvement of the monk in the choir, above all for an understanding of the themes, or subject matter, of the psalms. In Stephen's view, the best method to pray the psalms is not to strain oneself by making all kinds of mental efforts, but to concentrate on the very themes of the psalms and then apply these themes to Christ and the individual soul.

A proper understanding of the psalms is therefore indispensable. While Stephen was acquainted with the contemporary exegetical methods—the literal, mystical, moral, and anagogical interpretations of the Bible—in his wish to write primarily for beginners and the simple-hearted who needed simpler approaches to the psalmody, he opted for the literal meaning of the psalms whenever they related an event in the Old Testament. But given the economy of salvation—man's creation by God, his recreation through the Incarnation, his justification through the sacraments, and his glorification in heaven—he realized the need for other exegetical methods and resorted, therefore, above all to the mystical interpretation when pondering God's goodness and his efforts on behalf of man's salvation.

To demonstrate his point, Stephen offered a verse-by-verse commentary on Psalms 3 and 94 (the invitatory at Matins), the hymn *Aeterne rerum Conditor* of Sunday Matins and Psalm 20. But since he was unable to give a similarly detailed exegesis of the entire psalter, he merely indicated the themes of the other psalms as they follow in the Cistercian office. They center on God, the Old and New Testaments, the pilgrim Church, the vicissitudes of saints and sinners, the persecution of the good, the soul's longing for the life to come, and eternal glory.

While the themes of the Canticles recited during Lauds are briefly indicated, nothing is said about the prayer, or collect, which today concludes every canonical hour, nor is any reference made to the Office of the Virgin Mary or the Office of the Dead; the author, as he himself admitted, simply did not have the time for an expanded treatment of his subject.

As a man of experience, Stephen proposed a number of practical ways to understand the psalmody. In some instances one must apply the psalms or verses within a psalm to Christ himself, in other cases to the individual soul. To overcome difficulties and distractions during the psalmody, the monk should focus his eyes on the floor in front of himself and picture Christ as if he were present, and while standing with his elbows resting on the choir stalls, he should see himself as if he were suspended on the cross, and draw inspiration from this.

The conclusion summarizes the beauty and the fruits of the divine office. Because the monk does not simply rely on his own strength but builds on the work of Christ and his glorious deeds, his prayer will certainly be pleasing to God; hence the psalmody is and will always be a more fruitful exercise than any private prayer. The importance of the treatise is thus well established. It is the only writing of its kind on the psalmody by a medieval Cistercian author which upholds the importance of the divine office as a community exercise in a wholly supernatural atmosphere.

Taken together, Stephen's purported writings tend to form a certain unit. The four titles comprise a spiritual teaching which includes every important aspect of the spiritual life. But instead of concentrating on negatives, on attitudes to be changed and vices to be combatted, Stephen stressed the positive motives of the spiritual life: the goodness of God, the great deeds of the Saviour, the ministrations of angels, the mediation of Mary, the intercession and glory of the saints, and the noble and tender feelings of the human heart capable of great initiatives. Such an approach, based on fundamental and joyful truths, has an enduring value.

Bede K. Lackner, O. CIST.

University of Texas—Arlington

NOTES TO INTRODUCTION

1. *Revue d'ascétique et de mystique* 10 (1929) 368–415.
2. *RAM* 11 (1930) 355–374.
3. *Collectanea O.C.R.* 8 (1946) 17–68.
4. *Cîteaux* 23 (1972) 245–288.
5. See André Wilmart, *Auteurs spirituels et textes dévôts du moyen âge* (Paris, 1932) 317–360, and *Dictionnaire de Spiritualité* 4:1521–1524.
6. Vulgate enumeration, which has been followed throughout this volume.
7. In preparation by Dr O'Sullivan before his death and being edited by another of his students, Dr Anne Mannion —ed.

MEDITATIONS

MEDITATIONS

HERE BEGIN THE MEDITATIONS on the joys of the blessed and ever-glorious Virgin Mary, written by Stephen, venerable Abbot of Salley, in answer to a request made to him by a monk.*

The meditations are divided into three groups of five each, the group of fifteen being a type of the Canticle of the Fifteen Steps†[1] which the Virgin Mary, only three years old, is said to have mounted without being held or supported by human hands when she was led by her parents into the Temple to enter God's service in accordance with his will, which was revealed by the angel who announced the conception of Christ. Each of the fifteen meditations include: a meditation on the particular Joy; a statement of that Joy addressed directly to the Virgin; a petition by the meditator; and the 'Hail Mary', supplemented by certain words of love. After the fifth and the tenth petition of the first and second group [of five meditations] there are two pauses recapitulating the thoughts of the meditator.

My dear friend; you are a man whose demands are great.* You still insist upon asking me to put for you in writing form, briefly, some muttering on the prerogative Joys of Mary*[2] the most holy Mother of God, so that your mind can be roused and

*claustralis—
a simple monk to whom for one reason or other—most likely for no reason at all—no official burdens of office had been confided.*

†The Gradual Psalms, 119-133.

Dan 10:11

Cf. Bernard, O Asspt 2; SBOp 5: 262-74.

27

activated in the love of this most blessed
Virgin. Your continued entreaties made me
all the more uneasy the more I realized that it
is not proper for me to feel any essence of
joy. For, what should I have to do with joy?
Stained by sin, I must rather weep than write
about joy. As the wise man said, 'Inopportune
Sir 22:6   talk is like a song in time of mourning'.*

Yet, after God; all my spiritual comfort,
my life, my happiness, and hope depend on
From the final   this most gracious Virgin.* The more I am
Compline antiphon, aware that I have no merits of my own, that
Salve Regina.   much more must I look for the help of the
Mother of Mercy. Therefore, though I am her
unworthy servant and lacking in knowledge,
I shall in her honor and praise state what I
feel to be the best of my ability for the edifi-
cation of the young, without prejudice to
those of better spiritual understanding or
practical experience.[3]

Before all else you must understand this:
the tenderness, affection, and joy with which
the Blessed Virgin loved[4] her Son escapes and
Amadeus, Hom 4; transcends all human experience.* About this
SCh 72:130;   experience she could say, 'My secret belongs
CF 18:95   to me alone, my secret belongs to me
alone'; or 'My beloved belongs to me and I to
Sg 2:16.   him'.* From this it follows, since nobody
Cf. Is 24:16.   completely understood these joys, that different persons meditate in different ways
about them. Some compress them into one
group of five meditations, some into seven,
and then there are those who stretch them
out to twenty. But, if it pleases you, my dear
friend, I shall divide the prerogatives of the
Virgin's joys into three groups of five

meditations, taking into consideration that not a few people are rather busy and that too much abundance breeds aversion. Thus, if you have no time to complete all the meditations, you can pause after each group. The first group of five shall cover the period from the Virgin's birth to the birth of Christ; the second, from the birth of the Saviour to his crucifixion; the third, from the passion to the assumption of the Blessed Virgin.

It is only right and proper that I should begin the Joys with the birth of the blessed Mother of God whose holy and singular birth brought joy to the whole world.* Accordingly, construct the first meditation on her birth in the following manner.

Cf. Bernard, Nat BVM; SBOp 5:278-9. Amadeus, Hom 2; SCh 72: 68-86; CF 18: 69-75.

FIRST GROUP
FIRST MEDITATION

Ponder on the wretched state of the world from the days of Adam until the coming of Christ when death reigned,* when sin and evil held sway over the earth, enshrouding all mankind in the darkness of ignorance and despair so that every holy man, every just man and innocent man, and even John the Baptist, went down into limbo's exile. But then, to those who were sitting in darkness and in the shadow of death,* the Virgin Mary came forth as does daylight out of darkness and as does the morning star out of dawn;* she brought salvation and dispelled the darkness and the clouds.* Thus, as blessed Bernard said, 'If you take the light-

Rom 5:14

Lk 1:79

Sg 6:9f.

Sir 50:6

Nat BVM;
SBOp 5:279

giving sun from the world, where then is the light of day? If you take Mary, the star of the sea, what is left but an inwrapping cloud, the shadow of death and impenetrable darkness?'*

Form in your mind a picture of this situation. See how this welcome event brought grace and hope to those who had lost hope, deliverance to those who had lost heart, light to those living in darkness, and freedom to those oppressed in a dark prison. Contemplating this joy, say:

First Joy

Rejoice, O most glorious Mother of God, Mary most holy and ever-virgin, because your birth brought joyful tidings to the whole world. To the souls in purgatory you brought liberation; to men on earth, salvation; to the angels in heaven, glory; and to the heavenly city, restoration.

First Petition

Sweet Lady, by the prerogative of this Joy, that is, the memory of your holy birth, enkindle my weak and confused mind with the light of spiritual desires, so that having cast aside the darkness of worldly pride, I may, through your intercession, be the recipient of the joys accruing from the vision of the eternal truth. O clement, O loving, O sweet Mary.

Hail, holy, glorious, perpetually loving Mother of God, Mary ever-virgin, full of grace. The Lord is with you. Blessed are you among women and blessed is the Lord Jesus, the sweet fruit of your blessed womb. Amen.

SECOND MEDITATION

The second meditation probes, after the consideration of her illustrious birth, the Virgin's celebrated life which enlightens the whole Church. It recalls with what labors and pure love the holy One of Sion bedecked her bridal chamber, the tabernacle of her body and heart, which alone among all womankind deserved to be the recipient of Christ the king. Admire her deep humility, her conscientious virginity, her tender love. Because of her humility she deserved to be called queen of heaven; because of her virginity, the immaculate mother of the virgin-born Son; because of her love, the Mother of Mercy.*[5]

O Holy Mother of God, truly you were begotten beautiful and lovely in the fullness of all virtues.* To yourself you drew the Son of God from his Father's bosom. As blessed Bernard exclaimed: 'Sweet Mother of Mercy, you brought to us in a wonderful way the king and lord of heaven. You somehow put a check on his unbridled power, so that the right hand of the King which was wont to strike down* and to show no pity is now, because of you, ever inclined to compassion and forgiveness'.* Contemplating this joy and prerogative say:

Second Joy

Rejoice, O most glorious Mother of God, Virgin Mary most holy, because your most holy life has illumined the whole world. Alone among the daughters of men, you vowed your virginity in gift to God—something unheard-of in the world until that time. Your action and

Cf. Bernard, Miss 2; SBOp 4: 21-3; CF 18:15-17

Amadeus, Hom 2; SCh 72:68,70; CF 18:69,70.

Jb 5:17f.

Bernard p Epi; SBOp 4:315, & Asspt 4; SBOp 5:249.

example is an invitation to all to imitate your
humility, your chastity, and your love.

Second Petition

O sweetest of virgins, by virtue of these your
inmost sentiments which made you of womankind alone pleasing without parallel to Jesus
Christ, strengthen my life in these virtues,
that when I depart from this world you will
recognize me, unworthy that I am, as one of
your servants.

Hail, holy, glorious, perpetually loving Virgin Mary, Mother of God, Mary ever-Virgin,
full of grace. The Lord is with you. Blessed
are you among women and blessed is the
Lord Jesus, the sweet fruit of your blessed
womb. Amen.

THIRD MEDITATION

This meditation deals with the archangel
Gabriel as he came down from heaven and,
gently greeting the Virgin, formulated the
sweet salutation in which the whole world
rejoices for all times to come.[6] My dear
friend, imagine and picture the wonder,* the
love and joy experienced by the Blessed
Virgin when the angel appeared and spoke to
her, when she heard the details of the coming
salvation and was comforted by the angel.
Weigh these thoughts from the gospel according to Luke, 'the Angel Gabriel was
sent . . . ' ,* to the passage where the Virgin
gave her assent. Considering all this, say:

Third Joy

Rejoice, O most glorious Mother of God, Mary
ever-Virgin, most holy, because you alone
were worthy to receive the joyful news of

Bernard: 'Turbata est, sed non perturbata'; SBOp 4:42.

Lk 1:26-28

salvation transmitted to you from heaven by
an angel.

Third Petition

Sweetest of ladies, teach me, I implore you,
by the joy of this singular salutation to offer
to you daily the gentle angelic salutation, this
first pledge of our salvation, with a heart full
of love and lips that are clean. Grant that it
may be a comfort in all my tribulations and a
remedy* in all my temptations—to your honor
and glory. O clement, O loving, O sweet Mary.

Hail, holy, glorious, perpetually Mother of
God, Mary ever-virgin, full of grace. The Lord
is with you. Blessed are you among women
and blessed is the Lord Jesus, the sweet fruit
of your blessed womb. Amen.

Bernard, Pen 2; SBOp 1:167.

FOURTH MEDITATION

The fourth meditation elevates the mind to
reflect on the saving deeds of the holy
Trinity:* God the Father, in his exceeding
love,† sent us his only begotten Son in the
flesh.** The Son, in his unspeakable mercy,
took upon himself our weaknesses,†† our
labors and sorrows and all the burdens of our
misery, with the exception of sin.* The
Holy Spirit, lovingly overshadowed the Vir-
gin† with a tenderness indescribable and set
her alight and ablaze so that, absolutely
beautiful in body and soul, her whole being
was aflame with love, like red hot gold in a
red hot furnace.** Once the surging flood of
divine power had placidly entered her virginal womb, she no longer thought the
thoughts of man. Gone from her was every
carnal thought; all she experienced was

Cf. Amadeus, Hom 3; SCh 72: 91; CF 18:78. FCh 25:409-410. See also St Augustine, Sermon 186 on the Feast of the Nativity, FCh 38:10.

†Eph 2:4.

**Rom 8:3. Cf. Hallier, Monastic Theology, 12-18, on Aelred's phrase 'land of unlikeness'.

††Mt 8:17.
*Heb 4:15.

†See Amadeus, Hom 3; SCh 72: 105; CF 18:84.

**Ibid.; 108, 86.

grace in its fullness

Enchanted with this sweetness, think in your ecstasy and jubilation of the singular intervention of the Holy Spirit, when our Lord Jesus Christ, the Son of God, was conceived in this virginal womb. Think how the Holy One was conceived from the holy Virgin, the sinless One from the stainless Virgin, the one and only Son from the one and only Virgin.

Who can sufficiently estimate the fullness of the joy with which Majesty Itself—the Trinity—wrought the salvation of the whole human race* in the womb of the Virgin Mary. As blessed Bernard expressed it, 'As all things look to their respective center, so the souls in purgatory look to Mary for deliverance; the souls in heaven, that their glory be complete and men on earth, that they may be saved.'*

I say this in my ignorance and lack of experience: I do not think that the blessed Virgin experienced a joy greater [than this] during her earthly life. In remembrance of this Joy, say:

Fourth Joy

Rejoice, O most glorious Mother of God, Mary most holy and ever-Virgin, because through the intervention of the Holy Spirit you conceived Our Lord Jesus Christ, true God and true man, in your chaste womb. You experienced all the joys of motherhood and, at the same time, the honor of being a virgin. There is none like you among the former nor will you ever have an equal among the latter.*

Ps 73:12.
Cf. SBOp 5:167.

Pent 2; SBOp
5:167-8.

1 Kgs 3:12. Cf.
Bernard, O Asspt;
SBOp 5:269.

Fourth Petition

Sweetest of ladies, through the unfathomable joy of your gentle soul make me ever mindful of this great abundance of sweetness and joy. Help me to keep its memory in my heart for the good of my soul and on my lips for the consolation of my life. Through your constant intercession, O kindest Mother of Mercy, let Jesus, your sweetness, be honey in my mouth, melody in my ear, jubilation in my heart. O clement, O loving, O sweet Mary.

Hail, holy, glorious, and perpetually loving Mother of God, Mary ever-Virgin, full of grace. The Lord is with you. Blessed are you among women and blessed is the Lord Jesus, the sweet fruit of your blessed womb. Amen.

FIFTH MEDITATION

During the fifth meditation bear in mind that the more exalted the blessed Virgin became as the Mother of the only-begotten Son of God, the queen of heaven and the mistress of the world, the more she humbled herself. She crossed the mountain [of Judaea] to greet and serve Elizabeth in greatest humility.* This is why Elizabeth, filled with the   *Lk 1:39* Holy Spirit, cried out, 'Who am I that the Mother of my Lord should come to me?'*   *Lk 1:43.*

Visualize the nature and greatness of this joy when upon the mere salutation of the Virgin* the mother [of John] began to   *Lk 1:41.* prophesy, the Precursor, still enclosed in her womb, leapt for joy,* and the soul of the   *Ibid.* sweet Virgin magnified the Lord.* Reflecting   *Lk 1:46-55* on these blessed joys of the two mothers and on the singular communication of the holy infants still in their mothers' wombs, say:

Fifth Joy

Rejoice, of most glorious Mother of God, Mary ever-Virgin, most holy because by your mere greetings you filled Elizabeth and John with unspeakable joy.

Fifth Petition

Sweetest of ladies, recalling the Joy you felt in your soul when Elizabeth called you blessed among women and called the fruit of your womb blessed, because you believed* in the salvation of the whole human race, I implore your help. As your own spirit rejoiced in God, your Saviour,* so let your words be sweeter than all else to my sinful ears.* Pour the drops of your grace into my parched soul so that, well grounded in true humility, I may be able to serve you with my whole being.

Hail, holy, glorious, perpetually loving Mother of God, Mary ever-virgin, full of grace. The Lord is with you. Blessed are you among women and blessed is the Lord Jesus, the sweet fruit of your blessed womb. Amen.

FIRST PAUSE

Now make the first pause, but in such a way that you will not be idle during this rest period. On the contrary, use it to think about the virtues of the glorious Virgin and how she deserved to become the couch for 'the fullness of deity'. In the sanctuary of her most holy body, the source of all creatures, the glory and splendor of the Father, true light from true light, chose to dwell for nine months. How happy is she who experienced fully

Lk 1:45

Lk 1:47.

Sg 2:14

within herself what the whole world could not understand. Who can fully measure the joy and the love, the loving thoughts, and the pure ecstasy of the blessed Virgin when she felt the movement of her beloved Son in her virginal womb? Or her delight that the fountain of sweetness deigned to be a guest in her womb over a nine-month period? In her dwelt—so-to-say, corporeally,* —'the fullness of deity'. Thoughts such as these will place you in a joyful disposition.†

Col 2:9. Cf. Amadeus, Hom 3; SCh 72:92-4; CF 18:80.
†Ps 75:11.

SECOND GROUP
SIXTH MEDITATION[7]

Proceed in due time to the sixth meditation. Contemplate to your soul's delight* the starting point of our salvation, the immaculate birth—a birth from which the Light and Life,* the Maker of the world, a man beautiful in form beyond the sons of men, came forth from her bridal chamber.* Behold the Mother's virginal integrity* though she had given birth, but even more, the godhead of the newborn Child and the mystery of the incarnation.* Think in wonderment of the angels sa they announced the great Joy to the shepherds, and of the shepherds as they hastened to see the Word Incarnate, the newborn Saviour of the world.

Pr 29:17

Jb 3:20

Ps 44:3; 18:6.

*Cf. Amadeus, Hom 3:SCh 72:100; CF 18:83. FCh 38:25.

*Cf. Amadeus. Hom 3; SCh 72:94; CF 18:80.

Look at the Word, yelping in the manger; look at the Word, through whom all things came into being in the beginning; the Word, clad in the light which clothes the angels in heaven, now wrapped in swaddling clothes. O infant filled with wisdom, O Word

Incarnate whimpering, O humble majesty,
O noble infirmity! O blessed shepherds who
deserved to witness such great mysteries! But,
more fortunate still is the Virgin, chosen not
only to contain in her womb God, the
Container of all things, but also to fondle him
at her bosom, to hold him in sweet embrace,
to kiss his holy lips and to comfort him
with her breasts filled from heaven.

Fortunate is the soul which is privileged to
ruminate on these matters, which is allowed
to look with a loving heart on the child Jesus
wrapped in swaddling clothes, placed in a
manger and exposed to the animals, while
angels stand in readiness to wait on him.
Happy is the soul which can picture Joseph
benumbed by this great new miracle, or
visualize Mary lying on her side because of
her Son's needs or the Child lying in the
middle of animals, looking at the angels and
smiling at his parents. But even greater is the
joy of the Mother, for she could touch his
sacred limbs, hold his holy arms, and kiss his
holy mouth as often as she wished. These
physical acts further enflamed her soul once
he whom she carried for nine months in her
heart and womb increased her motherly joys
with his physical presence. He was near her to
be embraced and present to be kissed. Recalling this sublime and singular Joy, say:

Sixth Joy

Rejoice, O most glorious Mother of God,
Mary most holy, ever-virgin. A virgin before,
during and after giving birth, you gave the
world the new joy, Our Lord Jesus Christ,
the blessed fruit of your womb, the Saviour

and Deliverer of our souls.

Sixth Petition

O sweetest of ladies, by virtue of the incomparable birth whereby you gave us the son of the Creator of all things, and in the name,* the love and goodness of your most beloved son, I implore you, through the constant reminder of this meditation, to arouse in me a tenderness of heart, that I may avoid all lapses into slothfulness. Let me return to your precious birth, your motherly affections and cares during the tender infancy of your son as to a breast where I will learn to love in tenderness your beloved Son to whom you, his dear mother, tendered sweet breasts, thus giving to us wretches not drops of myrrh,* but the choicest mercies to this day, so that you are properly called Mother of Mercy. O clement, O loving, O sweet Mary.

Cf. Bernard, SC 15; SBOp 1: 82-8; CF 4:105-13. Cf. Bernard, Circ 1; SBOp 4: 275.

Sg 5:13.

Hail, holy, glorious, perpetually loving Mother of God, Mary ever-virgin, full of grace. The Lord is with you. Blessed are you among women and blessed is the Lord Jesus, the sweet fruit of your blessed womb. Amen.

SEVENTH MEDITATION

In the seventh meditation think of the Magi* as they journeyed from the East, following the star of grace which enlightens from within. Seeking Jesus in Jerusalem, they located him in Bethlehem in the palace made by his own choosing, that is, in a cheap and shabby rooming house. As Matthew says, 'They found him with Mary, his mother',* whimpering in the manger or at repose in his mother's lap, drinking at her breasts, stretched out in the

Cf. Bernard, Epi 2: SBOp 4:300-304.

Mt 2:11

Mt 2:11

ell of her arm, ready so-to-say to be kissed. 'And falling down they adored him.'* They adored the Word in the flesh, wisdom in a child, power in apparent weakness, the majesty of the Godhead in the very reality of a human being. Happy the finding of the infant Jesus with Mary his mother! Happy the adoration of the Godhead in a man.* Happy the Magi so enlightened by divine grace that him whom they acknowledged as One God by their adoration they proclaimed as the Trinity by threefold gifts:† *gold* acknowledged the Father's power; *myrrh,* the Son's wisdom and his assumed mortality; *incense* symbolized the Holy Spirit, who is love and tenderness of the Father and the Son. Through his breath breathe all the needy. Where a Mother has so many joys, who can name the sweetest among them, especially when they are joys of the soul? In admiration of this Joy, say:

*Cf. Bernard, Epi 3; SBOp 4: 305-7. Cf. Augustine, Sermons 190 and 200 on the epiphany; FCh 58:59,67.
†SBOp 4:306-7.

Seventh Joy

Rejoice, most glorious Mother of God, most sweet Mary, ever-virgin, because your eyes gazed in happy wonder at the shining star and saw the Magi approaching on their journey. You offered your Son to them for adoration and understood in your soul the mystical meaning of the three gifts.[8]

Seventh Petition

O clement, O loving, O sweet Mary, sweetest of all ladies, by virtue of the holy joys which overcame you as you watched your child play with his rattles and toys, I beg you to enlighten my mind so that, taught by the Magi, I may always long for you, always attend you lovingly and thus deserve to find near you my Lord Jesus, the blessed fruit of your womb, who is good, gentle, and merciful, resting in your arms, at your breast, or in your lap. Grant that, with you as my patron, I may worthily present to him these mystical gifts: the choicest *myrrh,** that is, complete mortification of the flesh; the *incense* of fervent prayer, and the *gold* of true discretion.

Sg 5:5

Hail, holy, glorious, perpetually loving Mother of God, Mary ever-virgin, full of grace. The Lord is with you. Blessed are you among women and blessed is the Lord Jesus, the sweet fruit of your blessed womb. Amen.

EIGHTH MEDITATION

In the eighth meditation focus your mind on the Mother of God as she carried in her loving arms the Lord of the temple to the temple of the Lord, there to offer to God the Father the first fruit of the human race.* Form a mental picture of the Church triumphant as it rushes to the aid of the Church militant so that with the true Solomon placed between them,* angels and men may have one and the same shepherd.* This is the reason why the ceremony is called the solemnity of the purification or the Lord's meeting.[9]

1 Cor 15:23.
Cf. Bernard, Pur 1;
SBOp 4:334.

Cf. 1 Kgs 3:5.

Jn 10:16

In this meditation explore this marvelous mystery: on the one hand, there is the Virgin in her new radiance, but at the same time weighed down by her noble burden as she carried with her hands the Son who was before the daystar,* aware of the joys of her motherhood while not knowing herself to be a wife.* On the other hand, there is Simeon and Anna, the Law and Prophecy, receiving

Ps 109:3
Ps 112:9. Cf. Augustine, Sermon 187 on the nativity;
FCh 38:13.

joyfully the One promised of old—the true light sent by the Father in the light[10] of the virginal body filled with the Holy Spirit—prophesying the illumination of the gentiles

Lk 2:32.

and the glory of the people of Israel.*

In this meeting of angels and men, of Jews and Gentiles, of the Old and the New Law, who can worthily express the praises of Mary or fathom her joys? Who can understand the wonderful mysteries of this Purification? In bringing to mind this Joy, say:

Eighth Joy

O most glorious Mother of God, Mary most holy, ever-virgin, when you carried Our Lord Jesus Christ, the only-begotten Son of God and your first-born in your arms to the Temple of the Lord, you offered [him] —the new offering of man's salvation—to God the Father as the first pledge toward the reconciliation of the human race and the salvation of all the faithful.

Eighth Petition

O sweetest of ladies, by virtue of these your holy and sublime joys, I beg you to purge my soul, still journeying in the dark confines of my body, of all its impulses. Make it sigh after your most beloved Son that, guided by faith, it may become an offering to God the Father in his holy temple until, departing in

*Lk 2:29

†Mal 4:2.
Cf. Mal 3:20.*

peace,* it will deserve to contemplate the very Sun of Justice† with God the Father and the Holy Spirit, the one and only Light of the material and spiritual creation, in the eternal vision of the heavenly Jerusalem. O clement, O loving, O sweet Mary.

Hail,   holy,   glorious,   perpetually loving

Mother of God, Mary ever-virgin, full of grace. The Lord is with you. Blessed are you among women and blessed is the Lord Jesus, the sweet fruit of your blessed womb. Amen.

NINTH MEDITATION

The ninth meditation concentrates on the marvelous adult life of Jesus which followed his miracle-filled childhood. The first thing that comes to mind is what happened to him in the temple at the age of twelve, as it is recorded in the gospel: 'The child Jesus remained behind [in Jerusalem] unknown to his parents'.*

*Lk 2:43.
Cf. Aelred, Iesu;
SCh 60:57-63;
CF 2:3-39.

On this point picture to yourself what great sorrow befell the Virgin when she realized she had lost her Son; what anguish crushed those very bowels of mercy when she did not see the Beloved of her womb. Picture the great solicitude with which she sought him whom she loved above all else.* And how great was the happiness that overflooded her heart when, at the end of three days, she saw him, whom she loved to the very depths of her soul sitting in the midst of the learned, listening to them and asking them questions.* O blessed and most loving of virgins, what must have been going through your soul when you heard with your own ears the young boy, Jesus, expounding the Law to legal experts and men of learning, or discussing the non-observance of the Law with great erudition, and when you heard him disseminating the salutary teachings of the New Law and excelling in amazing debating skills.

What answer can be given to all this beyond

Sg 3:4

Lk 2:46

what is said in these words of the gospel: 'Mary treasured all these things and reflected on them in her heart'?*

Lk 2:19. Cf. Ael-
red, Iesu 9; SCh
60:67; CF 2:12-13.

O blessed concentration, contemplation, and understanding! Mary, sublimely and singularly purified and enlightened by the gift of understanding, comprehended and weighed in herself not only these words but all the things she heard in this life from her Son, the power and wisdom of God,* as she fully knew. She knew that not only his words but also his actions possessed a mystical significance.

1 Cor 1:24.

O blessed Virgin, did not your exceeding joy increase ineffably when the Son of God left what is his Father's business* and went down with you to Nazareth where he was subject to you and the carpenter?* About him you have read and you know what has been written: 'You have subjected all things under his feet'.* In remembrance of this Joy say:

Lk 2:49

Lk 2:51.

Ps 8:8

Ninth Joy

Rejoice, O most glorious Mother of God, Mary most holy, ever-virgin, because after the sorrow which resulted from the loss of your Son you were gladdened all the more when he was found in the Temple. You were delighted in the wisdom he displayed before all who were present. Rejoice also, because he humbly subjected himself to you and shared with you the same blessed home life.

Ninth Petition

O clement, O loving, O sweet Mary, sweetest of ladies, by the memory of this unspeakable joy, tear me away from all carnal pleasures and lead me in truly humble subjection. May your holy merits grow in me an appetite for your Son's words of wisdom which must be my daily food. Taught by them, I will learn to want my Lord Jesus wherever I go. I will grieve whenever I lose him and with you search for him in the *triduum* of my mind, my words, and my actions; and I shall not rest until I find him again, always under your guidance, O most glorious Virgin. O clement, O loving, O sweet Mary.

Hail, holy, glorious, perpetually loving Mother of God, Mary ever-virgin, full of grace. The Lord is with you. Blessed are you among women and blessed is the Lord Jesus, the sweet fruit of your blessed womb. Amen.

TENTH MEDITATION

The tenth meditation, which follows the meditation on wisdom, deals with the miracles of the Lord Jesus and the revelation of his power at the beginning of his public life. The conversion of water into wine marked the first of his miracles; it proved that he was the true God at whose command nature itself changed.* In this meditation think of the loving Mother as she begged her all-powerful Son to have mercy and compassion on their embarrassed hosts. It was then that he revealed the power of the Godhead and by this physical act he established one of the Church's sacraments. In matters such as these, who can fully express Mary's joys, extended beyond measure, when her beloved Son, hereto known almost to her, his mother, alone, revealed himself in public.* This he did in the following manner: on his mother's request, he

*Jn 2:11, Cf. Bernard, O Epi 2 (SBOp 4:430), SC 85, 12-13 (SBOp 4:430; CF 40:208-10), Isaac, O Epi (SCh 130:204-20; CF 11:73-80).

*Jn 21:1

changed water into wine. On the same day but
not in the same year, he bowed down for baptism at the hands of John; he made water holy
for us in baptism by its contact with his
sacred body, and he introduced to all mortals
the holy and undivided Trinity: the Father,
by his spoken word; the Son, by means of
his human presence; and the Holy Spirit,
under the appearance of a dove.*

In all these instances the Holy Mother of
God was filled with a joy which surpassed all
the joys experienced by any human being. In
remembrance of this Joy, say:

Tenth Joy

Rejoice, O most glorious Mother of God,
Mary ever-virgin, because you delighted in
those sweet joys which the childhood and the
wisdom of your Son wrought in your soul.
You rejoiced even more when, at the time of
his baptism, he revealed himself to the whole
world as true God and, at the same time,
manifested the Holy Trinity;* and you rejoiced when he changed water into wine and
performed other miracles.

Tenth Petition

Sweetest of ladies, mindful of your indescribable joy at your Son's miracles, I implore you
to prepare my impure heart so that, upon
your glorious intercession, the Holy Spirit
may in his kindness descend into it, make it
his abode,* and enlighten it by revealing the
Holy Trinity. May the ardor of the divine
presence turn the waters of empty chatter
and the passions of the flesh in me into the
wine of compunction; may they change the
waters of servile fear into the wine of love;

*Mt 3:15-17,
Mk 1:10-11,
Lk 3:22, Jn 1:
31,34. Cf. Ber-
nard, JB; SBOp
5:176-8.*

Mt 3:13-17

Jn 14:23

may they change the lukewarm waters of neglect and the turbulent waters of carelessness into the unadulterated wine of love and pure devotion—through your constant intercession on my behalf. O clement, O loving, O sweet Mary.

Hail, holy, glorious, perpetually loving Mother of God, Mary ever-virgin, full of grace. The Lord is with you. Blessed are you among women and blessed is the Lord Jesus, the sweet fruit of your blessed womb. Amen.

THIRD GROUP
SECOND PAUSE

During the second Pause think of the singular joys which the blessed Virgin Mary felt about the glorious deeds of Our Lord and Saviour from the time of his baptism to his passion, when he went about healing all and doing good.* Consider the raising up of the lame, *Ac 10:38* the cure of the blind and the sick, the healing of the deaf and the mute and, finally, the raising of Lazarus from the dead. And do not leave out the fast and temptation of the Lord, and his transfiguration on the mountain. Apply all these to your spiritual wounds, that is, to the sins of your soul, and implore most sincerely him who is simultaneously healer and healing* that, through his holy *Cf. Bernard,* words, he may cure the ills of your soul and *V Nat 4; SBOp* the desires of your flesh through the constant intercession of Mary, the ever-blessed Virgin and Mother of God.

ELEVENTH MEDITATION

In the eleventh meditation, consider the Son

of God at his eleventh hour, that is, at the
end of his life on earth, when he offered himself on the altar of the cross, suffering
though impassible and dying a slow death,
as the Virgin stood by with eyes full of love
and looked on at her only begotten Son, her
joy, in tortuous agony.

Who can rightly fathom the Mother's sorrow when she saw the precious body of her
Son, which she knew was most holy and free
of all blemish, stretched out on the wood of a
cross, and the head of Jesus, in whose
presence the angels trembled, crowned with
thorns; or when she saw his hands and feet
pierced with nails, his side split wide open by a
soldier's lance and a flow of blood running
down on every part of his body? Truly,
mother most loving, the sword of his suffering pierced through your soul.* Yet, despite
being wounded to the very depth of your being by a sorrow without comparison and
beyond description, you stood there as he
hung from the cross and witnessed how so
powerful, innocent, good and loving a Son was
put to so horrible a death by evil men. You
saw him lashed savagely by torturers; you
saw how irreverently he was reckoned among
thieves.* And yet despite your great anguish
and sorrow, did you not think of mercy—his
mercy—as he redeemed you and the whole
world? Did you not rejoice with unbounded
happiness, knowing with a faith that was certain and unshakeable that your Son's precious
blood had redeemed the whole world, that
hell had been despoiled, that the devil, though
strong, had been chained[11] and the door to

Lk 2:35. Cf. Ber-
nard, O Asspt;
SBOp 5:273.

Lk 22:37

the kingdom of heaven opened wide? Did
you not rejoice when you heard his tender
voice entrusting you to John, his beloved
disciple, so that a virgin would care for his
virgin mother?* For, whom did he value
more among those he left behind in this
world than John, to whose love he could
entrust so priceless a treasure of our hope
and salvation?

*Jn 19:26-27. Cf.
Oeuvres de St. Ber-
nard, 5:47. Cf. Guer-
ric, Asspt 4 (CF 32:
188), Amadeus,
Hom 6 (SCh 72:
164; CF 18:113).*

Who can fully describe your anguish during
your Son's passion, who can give an accurate
account of the joys of your heart in view of
our imminent salvation? Meditating on this
joy, say:

Eleventh Joy

Rejoice, O most glorious Mother of God,
Mary most holy, ever-virgin. You looked with
love-filled eyes at your Son hanging on the
cross; you saw his most pure body, conceived
in purity in a pure virgin, laid open for every
manner of beating; you looked on as he shed
that most precious blood which flowed un-
checked from all parts of his body and
washed away our sins; you watched him as he
freely accepted the death on the cross, thus
redeeming the whole world from the power
of the devil.

Eleventh Petition

O most clement Lady, by that most precious
blood which with eyes full of tears you saw
gushing from the wounds of your most beloved Son and by our own merits I implore
you to let me, the least worthy of your
servants, be among those who shall reap the
fruits of his glorious redemption so that,
cleansed from every stain of sin and washed

in the saving bath of salvation which flowed
as blood and water from his side,* I may, by
partaking of the sacrament of the altar, be
united to his mystical body in this life and
attain radiance through the glory of his resurrection in the life to come, through your
constant intercession. O clement, O loving,
O sweet Mary.

Hail, holy, glorious, perpetually loving
Mary, Mother of God, ever-virgin, full of
grace. The Lord is with you. Blessed are you
among women and blessed is the Lord Jesus,
the sweet fruit of your blessed womb. Amen.

TWELFTH MEDITATION

The twelfth meditation has as subject matter
that manifold and indescribable feeling of
joy* felt by the Blessed Virgin when she saw
that after such bitter suffering and the most
ignominious of deaths her beloved Son had
conquered the author of death and through
the victory of his glorious resurrection opened
the doors to the kingdom of heaven which
had been closed to humankind. It also considers the joy felt by the Blessed Virgin when
she heard that her Jesus had appeared to his
disciples, even though the doors of the room
in which they were staying were closed;*
that he offered his hands and his side to
be touched; that he triumphantly showed
them his glorified human body taken from
the Virgin Mother; that he made it quite plain
that he was given power over all in heaven and
on earth;* and that he strengthened their
faith during the following forty days by his

Jn 19:34

*Cf. Amadeus,
Hom 6; SCh 72:
158-64, esp 160;
CF 18:109-13,
esp 110.*

Jn 20:19

*Mt 28:18. Cf.
Hilary of Poitiers,
The Trinity,
FCh 25:469.*

numerous and truly comforting appearances.

Indeed, O Mother of Mercy, this blessed sight—when you saw and with your own eyes recognized your Son, the blessed fruit of your womb, in the glorified body of your flesh— filled your pious being completely with a joy greater than any man's joy. As great as was your sorrow over the death of your only begotten Son, greater still is now the joy and jubilation of your heart about his resurrection. As great as were your sorrows during his many sufferings, greater still is the joy he bestowed on your soul* by his glorious resurrection and apparition.

Ps 93:19. Cf. Amadeus, Hom 6; SCh 72:160,172- 80; CF 18:110, 115-8.

Twelfth Joy

Rejoice, O most glorious Mother of God, Mary virgin most holy, because following the enormity of your sorrows caused by the sufferings of your Son, you rejoiced with joy unmistakable about his glorious resurrection. During the next forty days he healed your sorrow and satisfied your longing by his miracles and his frequent and delightful apparitions.

Twelfth Petition

O most loving Comforter of the afflicted: Recalling his glorious resurrection I take refuge in you and with confidence beg you that, rising from the death of my soul through your holy intercession, I may also rise from the grave of evil habits in which I had lain weighed down for a long time, to the newness of a more holy life, so that I may attain heaven at the end of my life. Even if I could not be on hand to rejoice at these consolations, may I, in the meantime, at least

re-live them in my meory, with you as my
constant intercessor. O clement, O loving,
O sweet Mary.

Hail, holy, glorious, perpetually loving
Mother of God, Mary ever-virgin, full of
grace. The Lord is with you. Blessed are you
among women and blessed is the Lord Jesus,
the sweet fruit of your blessed womb. Amen.

THIRTEENTH MEDITATION

The thirteenth meditation considers the glory
surrounding the ascension of Our Lord, when
Christ's course of time on earth had run out,
when the business on which he journeyed
on earth and the mystery of our redemption
had been completed. It was then that Our
Saviour decreed to return whence he had

Eph 4:8f.   come; he ascended above all the heavens,* so
that all would be fulfilled.

Form in your mind a picture of the blessed
Mary as she stood with her women com-
panions on one side of the circle, while the
Apostles and all the disciples stood on the

Jewish custom   other,* and the Lord Jesus was standing in the
separates the sexes
at gatherings.   center. Picture him as he bade them a last
†Lk 24:50.   farewell, blessed them with raised hands† and
then ascended into heaven right before their
loving and tearful eyes.

At that moment, as the Lord had foretold,
Jn 16:6,20   sadness filled your hearts,* O blessed disci-
ples, as you saw your beloved Lord and loving
Master, for whom you had given up all things
and to whom you had transferred your alle-
Cf. Bernard, Asc 2;   giance and love, moving away bodily and
SBOp 127-8.   ascending into heaven.* If these sighs and
lamentations indicated the disciples' reactions

as they witnessed the departure of their
Master, how much greater and deeper must
have been the sorrows felt by the loving heart
of his mother Mary as she realized that she
was being left upon earth,* and that her son
Jesus, her one and only Joy, the complement
of her heart and of her whole life who could
not be separated from her heart and soul even
for a moment, was moving away before her
very eyes.

*Amadeus, Hom 7;
SCh 72:184;
CF 18:119.*

O Mary, my sweetest Life, how great and
anguished must have been your soul's longing
for his presence, to see him crowned with
honor and glory* by God the Father in
heaven! It is quite impossible for the human
heart to fathom your ineffable joy when,
receiving consolation after your tears and
longings, you saw with the eyes of the faith
the true body of your Son, taken from your
virginal body, raised above the highest heavenly hosts to the sublimity of God the
Father and placed on the throne of glory at
his right where he was to prepare for you, his
beloved Mother, a place of immortality.*
O joy unspoken, O truly holy and ecstatic
jubilation, as you beheld the progeny of your
holy womb, once spat on, flogged, and crucified, now sitting at the Father's side as his
co-equal. Contemplating this Joy, say:

Ps 8:6

**Mk 16:19; Col 3:1;
Heb 12:2; 1:3;
Jn 5:22-23. Cf.
Hilary of Poitiers,
The Trinity,
FCh 25:469.*

Thirteenth Joy

Rejoice, O most glorious Mother of God,
Mary ever-virgin, most holy, because with
your eyes you saw the ascent of your Son,
your own flesh, into heaven there to sit on the
right hand of the Father, to prepare for you,
his beloved Mother, a place of immortality,

and to make you a trusted intercessor and a concerned advocate pleading with amazingly effective arguments.

Thirteenth Petition

Sweetest of ladies, by this singular favor which you have received from God, obtain for me, the least of your servants, that, rejoicing in the memory of this Joy and picturing your loving Son, my mind may be lifted up into the kingdom which the glorious Author had entered before your very eyes. Grant also that he direct my desires toward him and pull me away from earthly enticements and activities, through your intercession, O Mother of Mercy, for whom it is not difficult to request whatever you wish to obtain.* O clement, O loving, O sweet Mary.

Cf. Amadeus, Hom 7; SCh 72: 202; CF 18:127f.

Hail, holy, glorious, perpetually loving Mother of God, Mary ever-virgin, full of grace. The Lord is with you. Blessed are you among women and blessed is the Lord Jesus, the sweet fruit of your blessed womb. Amen.

FOURTEENTH MEDITATION

In this fourteenth meditation visualize the holy assembly of the disciples as they sat in one room,* spending their time in prayer and fasting while they awaited in respectful quiet the One promised by the Father.* Picture the Holy Spirit, as he appeared visibly in the form of tongues of fire* and, more miraculously still, filled the hearts of the disciples, these clean receptacles, with a marvelous sweetness of understanding. Who among those present at that gathering could describe the Joy of the blessed Virgin who with them and

Ac 2:1

Lk 24:49

Ac 2:3-4

already before them experienced the fire of
love, and understood the power of the Spirit
descending from above?* *Ac 1:8. Cf. Jn 16:13*

Actually, my dearest Lady, the Holy Spirit
dwelt in the innermost recesses of your heart,
his special shrine, already long before. But
now he enlightened your soul with joy without
parallel when you saw him with your own
eyes coming in the form of tongues of fire on
the disciples and when you realized that in his
presence the hearts of the disciples were filled
with all graces so that through them he would
pour the flood-waters of knowledge and grace
over the whole world. It further increased
your joy, O sweetest Lady, that this was the
first mission of your Son after his ascension.
A tender gift, a loving pledge, the sweetest of
consolations, is the Paraclete as he proceeds
directly from the Father and the Son.* His *Cf. Augustine,
The Trinity,
FCh 45:190.*
procession from the Son enflamed Mary's
loving heart all the more because she so
greatly longed for her Son. In sweet remembrance of this Joy, say:

Fourteenth Joy

Rejoice, O most glorious Mother of God,
Mary ever-virgin, because you witnessed with
your own eyes the actual coming of the Holy
Spirit and the enlightenment of the Apostles;
also, because you experienced within yourself the tenderness of His love and foresaw
how the Gentiles would be enlightened by
the Apostles' teaching.

Fourteenth Petition

Most clement of ladies, recalling the sweet
consolation which the Holy Spirit poured into
your heart in a truly singular way, I implore

you to intercede with the Holy Spirit on my
behalf so that through your powerful prayers
and the power and fire with which he
inflamed the hearts of the disciples and made
them fluent in speech and aflame with love,
he may burn off the shame of my sins and
enlighten my mind so that I may gain a better
understanding of true wisdom, and my cold
heart will become a furnace of his love. O clement, O loving, O sweet Mary.

Hail, holy, glorious, perpetually loving
Mother of God, ever-virgin, full of grace. The
Lord is with you. Blessed are you among
women and blessed is the Lord Jesus, the
sweet fruit of your blessed womb. Amen.

FIFTEENTH MEDITATION

The fifteenth meditation considers the completion of the blessed Virgin's joys in this
life: how after the ineffable longing with
which the most pious of mothers longed for
her Son during that intervening time when
she was left in this world for our salvation
and for the enlightenment and consolation of
the apostles, she was gloriously assumed into
heaven by her Son.*

Cf. Amadeus, Hom 7; SCh 72:184; CF 18:119.

Think of the glorious king, the king of
heaven, in the real but glorified flesh of the
Virgin, as he arrived with an uncountable
heavenly host to visit his beloved Mother
and take her away from this world's laborious
journey. Think how he raised her beyond the
heights of the heavens* and seated her on the
right hand side of his throne of glory, where
she rules triumphantly forevermore together
with him and his angels as the lady of the

Cf. ibid.; 190;122.

world, the queen of heaven* and empress of
the angels—yet also as the hope of the
wretched and the reconciliation of sinners.[12]

Picture to yourself the Queen of Heaven*
sitting in the flesh on the right hand side of
her Son and dispatching with clearcut effi-
ciency, in the presence of the highest Judge,
the pleas and complaints of her clients* as
they continue to flood her with their requests day and night from this valley of tears.
See how she influences her Son's judgment
with a mother's love, pointing out to him the
chaste bosom on which she fondled and
rested him, and the breast filled with the milk
of heaven with which she nourished him; see
how she is acting as mediatrix pleading for
the salvation of her devoted people.

O kindest of ladies, as you sit face to face
with your Son in glory pleading even in behalf of the very wicked, what is there that he
will not grant you? Did he not pour the grace
that filled his own heart from all eternity into
your gentle heart so that the fullness of the
Godhead* would dwell in your womb?

O most clement Lady, I will be satisfied—
I will indeed be completely satisfied—if, by
way of intercession, you will just once turn
your beautiful face on the eyes of majesty—
God the Father—in my behalf. I have no fears
that the Father of all mercies* will not
receive me among his sons when I have before
him the Mother of Mercy as my advocate,[13]
pleading for me in matters where I have reason
to fear him.

Your blessed presence has made joyful
the entire City of God* where you rejoice

Cf. ibid.; 190;122.

*Cf. Amadeus, Hom
7; SCh 72:190,
198-204; CF 18:
122,125-8.*

*Cf. Amadeus, Hom
8; SCh 216; CF 133.*

*Col 2:9. Cf. Ber-
nard, Asspt 1,
SBOp 5:229.*

2 Cor 1:3

Ps 45:5.

Ps 67:4

and exult* before God as the ranks of the
heavenly court look on in wonder. With your
blessed eyes, more beautiful than those of any
other creature, you now contemplate God the
Father and the Son—truly yours, truly Lord,
and truly Son—the Son in the Father and the
Holy Spirit in both. There is the Holy Trinity,
your whole joy and exultation, your whole
delight, the love of your heart—one God,
redeeming and saving the whole human race
through his Son and through you.

Given the immensity of this Joy, which I
am quite incapable of understanding or putting into words, throw yourself at the feet of
the Queen of Mercy, residing on her throne of
glory and bid to her, so-to-speak, a last
farewell:

Fifteenth Joy

Rejoice, O most glorious Mother of God,
Mary ever-virgin, most holy, most fortunate
of all creatures, the one and only hope of all
human consolation and joy, because you were
the recipient of such great joys, delights, and
exultations. These the Fountain of wisdom
and knowledge, born of you, heaped upon you
as they had never before been bestowed on
any human being, in order to complete your
joys and perfect your singular happiness. On

Sg 3:11

this festive day of your heart,* you rejoiced
without measure when your beloved Son
came for you and, glorifying you in body and
soul, placed you on the highest throne at the
right hand of God the Father where in the presence of his majesty, you happily joined your
Son, the glorious King of the universe, who
received you, you who caressed him in your

arms and fondled him in the lap of your pure virginity, with loving embraces.

Fifteenth Petition

O clement, O loving, O sweet and radiant Mary, the Joy of the heavenly city, please do not cease to be mindful of me, your poor servant who joyfully recollects your Joys, but give me the grace of possessing your sweet name and the name of your son Jesus in my heart forever. Grant also that the pleasant and joyful memories evoked by these names will make all transitory delights grow vile and bitter. Working faithfully on my behalf in the presence of your Son, O loving advocate, make me tenderly long for your blessed and glorious presence so that I will seek no sweetness other than yours and feel no other joy, no other love, than yours. In the meanwhile, turn your eyes of mercy toward me so that when my period of exile on this earth comes to an end, I may deserve to see Jesus, the blessed fruit of your womb, in his glory.

Hail, holy, glorious, perpetually loving Mother of God, Mary ever-virgin, full of grace. The Lord is with you. Blessed are you among women and blessed is the Lord Jesus, the blessed fruit of your womb. Amen.

As you see, my dear friend, I have become foolish; but you have driven me to it.* Hence, *2 Cor 12:11* do not pass along this treatise to over-critical readers; nor should you, yourself, read it with overly great expectations.

I have divided the joys into three groups of five and each individual meditation into a meditation proper, a joy, and a prayer of petition, for this reason: when you have time aplenty, meditate; when you do not, then read at least the various joys and the petitions.

May I particularly ask you and others who will read this writing and recall the holy Virgin's Joys to be mindful of my lowliness and intercede with the Father of mercy on my behalf. Ask her to obtain for me, a most unworthy sinner, through her powerful prayers that her most holy Son, the very Splendor of the Father's glory who from all eternity had chosen her as his immaculate mother, as his beloved and dearest spouse and has already introduced her into the chamber of eternal

Sg 3:4 light* so that she might faithfully intercede before him for sinners, will deign to forgive all my offenses, which I have committed with such easy-going rashness.

Finally, may the well-known love and the sweet memory of the Blessed Mary, Virgin and Mother, erase and wipe it away completely whatever I have said with a lack of prudence or with insufficient devotion about her Joys. Amen.

HERE COME TO A HAPPY END
THE MEDITATIONS ON THE JOYS OF
THE BLESSED VIRGIN MARY.

NOTES TO MEDITATIONS

1.   The origin of the gradual psalms debate: some think they were sung on the Temple steps, others that they were sung along the line of march by pilgrims on the way to Jerusalem. See Amadeus of Lausanne, Homily 2, for Mary's dress and appearance SCh 72:81; CF 18:73.

2.   Bernard's sermon is a more fulsome expression of Mary's prerogatives than is Stephen's treatise. This is understandable because Stephen's work is but a short outline of his thoughts on this subject. Stephen is much in debt to St Bernard and to Amadeus of Lausanne's *Homilies,* and also to St Augustine's sermons 184-196 on the nativity (trans. Sr. M. Muldowney, in *Sermons on the Liturgical Seasons,* FCh 38:3-47.

3.   Amédée Hallier, *The Monastic Theology of Aelred of Rievaulx,* CS 2 (1969) 116, 122. Chapter V of this study should be read for a better understanding of Stephen's words. Cf. Aelred of Rievaulx, Inst incl 27-28; SCh 76:106-114; CF 2:74-8.

4.   *Quo afficiebatur beata Virgo.* In medieval Latin the classical meaning of *afficere* and *affectus* had undergone a transformation in meaning. See Hallier, *Monastic Theology,* 25-55. See also D. Vitalis Lehodey, *The Ways of Mental Prayer* (Dublin, 1949), pp. 178-189.

5.   On the origin of cistercian devotion to the Mother of Mercy, see Marcel Aubert, *L'architecture cistercienne en France* (Paris, 1947) 24-25.

6.   This is the subject of St Bernard's four homilies, *In laudibus virginis matris,* more familiarly known as *Sermones in* Missus est; SBOp 4:13-58. See also Amadeus of Lausanne, Homily 3; SCh 72: 86-109; CF 18:77-86.

7.   This meditation relies heavily on St Bernard's *In laudibus virginis matris,* SBOp 4:13-58; portions are a paraphrase of St Augustine's Sermon 188.2 *On the Nativity,* in *Sermons on the Liturgical Seasons,* FCh 38:18-19.

8.   For a fuller discourse on this phrase: see *Oeuvres de St Bernard,* trans. M. S. Ravelet (Bar-le-Duc, 1870) 5:689, which is a treatise on the feast of the Epiphany attributed to Guerric, abbot of Igny (*Sermo I in Epiphaniam*).

9.   According to the Mosaic Law, Mary was unclean because she had given birth to a child. For a period of forty days she could not go to the

Temple. Only Mary had to be purified, but Jesus had to be redeemed. They made the offering of the poor—two turtledoves or two young pigeons. Here they met Simeon and Anna, thus the feast is known among the Greeks as *Hypapante,* The Meeting [of the Lord at the Purification]. It is called *Occursus Domini* or *Obvatio Domini* in the roman rite: both have the same meaning—meeting Jesus and Mary with Simeon and Anna. Cf. Bernard, Pur 3; SBOp 4:341-344.

10.   The *lucerna* was a brass vase used at ceremonies of the altar; it was also the occasionally used term for a thurible. John the Baptist is referred to as *lucerna ardens et lucens,* 'a burning and shining light' (Jn 5:38) by St Bernard, *Sermo in nativitate Johannis Baptistae;* SBOp 5:176-84, esp. 177-8.

11.   See Emile Mâle, *L'art réligieux du XIIe siècle en France* (Paris, 1924), p. 368 for a representation of the devil being held prisoner by an angel.

12.   The 'propitiatory' was the jewish 'seat of mercy', hence its application to the Blessed Virgin as the one who sat in that seat.

13.   This and several other phrases here are borrowed from the antiphon *Salve Regina* which concludes Compline and the monastic day.

A THREEFOLD
EXERCISE

A THREEFOLD EXERCISE

MY DEAR FRIEND; you asked me for the benefit of the young to commit to writing what I have said to you briefly and cursorily when we were discussing methods of prayer and meditation. Your request was, quite naturally, an annoyance to me when I first received it, mainly because the kinds of spiritual exercises you have in mind lean more in the direction of unspoken reflection than to the spoken word, or, I could say, they are more spoken of than written about. Also, my own very limited experience leads me to say, it is not easy to find a temptation which discourages, distracts, and more quickly confounds* the young in the rapture of prayer*—that is, souls who are experiencing the first stages of glowing in the embrace of the Spouse—than the suggestion that they somehow reveal to others their spiritual struggles. For such reason the Law prohibited work with the firstling of the bullock and the shearing of the first-born sheep.*

Jer 1:10

Ps 67:28

Deut 15:19

In view of all this I have feigned ignorance and maintained silence until now.* But because I did not forget your request and I am mindful of my promise to you, I shall fulfill your request insofar as I am able to do so. However, do not expect elegant style and composition, for one must say little in such a matter, so that what cannot be fully ex-

Jb 3:26

pressed in words may be better understood.

FIRST MEDITATION

At your first opportunity, at any hour of the
day or night, chase from your heart all carnal
imaginings and lift your mind up to the one
supreme principle and creator of all things:
God the Father, God the Son, and God the
Holy Spirit. Do this not as an intellectual
exercise, to comprehend him, as it were, or to
satisfy your curiosity, but through faith.
Thank God for all his blessings, both special
and general. For God is goodness itself,
supremely happy, powerful, and blessed. He
needs not anything,* living as he does in
unapproachable light.† His joy can neither
be increased nor diminished. Out of his goodness alone he revealed himself and created a
rational creature to be a gratuitous sharer of
his glory. Praise the Lord, therefore, for he is
good.* Give him thanks because he made you
a noble creature fashioned in his own image
and likeness,* with will, reason, and memory.* Love him with your whole heart and
your whole mind;† wholly cling to him and
to him alone.**

As Solomon said in Ecclesiastes, 'Truly,
Lord, you have made man upright'.* in the
state of innocence. You have made him immortal, able not to die, and pure, that is,
without carnal appetite, without any urge
impelling him toward sin. But man entangled
himself in an infinity of problems:* sorrows,
desires, interests, fears, black ignorance, the
doom of death, and countless other miseries
of both body and soul.

*Cf. Augustine,
Confessions,
FCh 21:5-6.
†1 Tim 6:16

Pss 106:1;
117:1; 135:1.

Gen 1:26

*Cf. Augustine,
Confessions,
FCh 21:295.
†Mt 22:37.
**Ps 72:28.

Qo 7:30

Ibid. 7:30

Start thinking, my dear friend, and formulate in your mind the causes, circumstances, and consequences of these facts. Ask for instance: whence and from whom did you fall. You fell from the paradise of delights* into banishment and punishment, from a place of pleasure† into a valley of tears.** With Jeremiah, see your fate in this valley. Ponder how mercifully and kindly, on no antecessory merits of your own, the good Lord has cleansed you of the filth of original sin in the sacrament of baptism and made you from a son begotten in anger* into a son of grace.

*Gen 2:8.
Gardens of Delight *were popular in the Middle Ages.*
†Gen 2:10.
**Ps 83:7.

Eph 2:3

Think also how, after reaching the age of reason, you have repaid your Creator with evil for good,* and with contempt—let me not say hatred—for love.* Recall in the bitterness of your soul* all your past sins: the number and kind of sins you have committed in a particular year or at a particular age; how many and what kind of sins you have committed in another year and at a more mature age; how, with heinous acts* of the body and evil deeds and blasphemies of the soul, you have offended God* your benefactor, who is kind and overlooks all sins so that men may repent.*

Ps 34:12
Ps 108:5.
Is 38:15.

*Cf. Augustine, Confessions, FCh 21:33.
*Deut 4:25.

Wis 11:41; Job 3:26.

Admire God's patience; wonder how that greatest of powers pretends not to see things over so long a time. Wonder at your own blindness; how a wretched creature like you could dare to perpetrate such enormous crimes in the sight of its Judge and the holy angels. Accept God's judgment, because you did not choose to refrain from sin when you

were able to do so and you cannot now that
you wish to do so.

Arousing yourself to compunction and
tears with such thoughts and self-accusations,
confess your sins daily to the Lord God. Confess them at least in a general way, but mention your graver sins specifically. After this
confession, raise your eyes to the triune God
in hopes of forgiveness and ask him with all
your fervor to look upon you in his mercy.
Beg him to restore by his power your own
poor 'trinity': your lifeless and weak *will*,
which revels in abominations of the flesh;
your errant, dissembling, and blind *reason*,
which enshrouds your spirit; and your busy,
distracted, and confused *memory*, which
fluctuates in temporal matters, that with
St Augustine you may be able to say: O
Lord, 'if I would only think of you—I would
understand you and love you!'*

The Trinity,
FCh 45:524.

Yes, let me love you—Father, Son, and
Holy Spirit—with my whole heart, my whole
soul, and my whole mind; let me love you
sweetly, wisely, and perseveringly.* Let me
love you, God the Holy Spirit, God of love
and sweetness, with my whole heart, that is,
with my whole will and with a tender and ex-
clusive love. Let me love you, God the Son,
God of wisdom, with my whole soul, that is,
with my whole mind and with a wise and
unshakeable love. Let me love you, God the
Father, God of power, of eternity and might,
with my whole mind, that is, with all my
thoughts and with a persevering and unchanging love. As St Augustine said in his *Confessions*, 'Let me love you entirely with my

whole self'.*

On finishing this meditation, not with the same words but with words given you from above—or, what I would prefer, with affections alone and no words—you may add the verse Glory be to the Father and to the Son and to the Holy Spirit and the hymn, 'We invoke you, we praise you, we bless you, we adore you, we glorify you, we long to serve you alone, O Holy Trinity'.* Say this three times, genuflecting in each instance. Then add the invocation, 'Let us bless the Father, the Son and the Holy Spirit', and the prayer 'Almighty and eternal God, you gave your faithful people . . .'.*

Confessions 33, FCh 21:452. Cf. Bernard, Dil 6; SBOp 3:124.

*Cf. Dan 3:26 ff., Alcuin, PL 101:56.

Collect of Trinity Sunday.

SECOND MEDITATION

In the second meditation, approach with confidence the throne* of the Mother of Mercy.* Think and consider how gloriously and happily the Blessed Virgin Mary sits as a crowned queen, raised above all the choirs of angels,* on the right hand side of her Son, as a lady, mother, and advocate. As Our Lady she can, as mother she wishes, as our advocate, she must come to our aid.

Indeed, sweet lady, you alone have been singled out among the race of women in the world, in you alone has wisdom built its house* that you would be mindful of human misery and frailty before God and faithfully intercede for us as our powerful lady, our loving mother, and our prudent and faithful advocate.

'Blessed is the soul,' says St Bernard,* 'which has the Son as its mediator before the

Heb 4:16.

*Cf. Salvre Regina, mater misericordiae, final antiphon at Compline.

*Antiphon at Sext on the Feast of the Assumption.

Pr 9:1.

*In fact, Ernaldus, De laudibus beatae Mariae Virginis, 189:1726. See Mikkers, RAM 11, (1930) 365 n. 33.

Father, and the Mother as its intercessor before the Son. Christ, baring his side, shows his wounds to the Father. Mary offers to Christ her virginal breasts and her nipples filled with heaven. She will not be refused anything since in her and through her flow these vessels of mercy. Mother and Son jointly pursue the work of salvation before the Father. Both argue in support of man's redemption with glorious claims and jointly secure the firm legacy of his reconciliation.[1] Mary unceasingly pleads with Christ, asking for the salvation of the world; the Son obtains salvation, the Father grants it.'

Dwell on the prospect of so glorious an intercession. Relish all its aspects and express your affectionate love of the sweetest of virgins with these or similar words:*

'O blessed discoverer of grace,* begetter of life and mother of salvation, by you we have access to your Son. May he whom you have given to us receive us through your intercession.* May your purity excuse in his sight the stain of our impurity, and may your humility, so dear to God, obtain forgiveness of our pride. May your overflowing love cancel the multitude of our sins.* And may your glorious fertility secure for us an abundance of merits.

Our Lady, our Mother, our Mediatrix and Advocate, reconcile us with your Son, recommend us to your Son, present us to your Son. Grant, O Blessed Lady, by the grace you have found, by the prerogative you have merited, by the mercy to which you have given birth, that he who through you has deigned to share

Cf. Bernard, Adv 2; SBOp 4:174.
*Cf. Bernard, Ep 174, (The Letters of St Bernard of Clairvaux, _trans._ Bruno Scott James [Chicago, 1953] 290—letter 215).
*Cf. Antiphon at Matins, Feast of St Andrew, 30 November.
Jm 5:20.

our weakness and misery may through your
intercession also make us participants of his
radiance and glory.

'You are full of grace,* you are covered
with the dew of heaven,† affluent in delights,
leaning on your Beloved.** Sweetest of virgins, feed my poor starved soul.* Feed it
from the abundant overflowing jug of your
grace,* that it may at last rejoice and take
root in your slow and gentle rain.* You are
truly the maiden pre-elected and prepared for
the Son of the Most High, the Lord Jesus
Christ, who loved and blessed you more than
anyone else by clothing you in a robe of
glory, by placing on your head a crown of
beauty,* the diadem of the kingdom of
heaven, and by having you sit at the right
[hand] side of the Majesty in heaven where
you, O loving Virgin, are never unmindful of
those who are mindful of you.'

In the quiet contemplation of this glorious
meditation, prostrate at the feet of this most
sweet Lady as if she were present, and say
with heart and soul, 'Hail, holy Queen,
Mother [of Mercy] . . . ' . Ask leave at the
beginning and say and formulate every word
in your heart as if you were in her presence.
Then add the verse, 'Pray for us, O holy
Mother of God . . . ' with a genuflection, and
the collect 'O God, you gave your people the
grace of eternal salvation . . . ' * which ends
with the words 'that she who gave us the
Author of Life while on earth, may in heaven intercede on our behalf.'

*Cf. Bernard,
o Asspt; SBOp
5:274.
†Sg 5:2.
**Sg 8:5.
*Lam 2:19.

Gen 24:20.

Ps 64:11.

*Is 28:5, cf. Sir
6:32.

*Collect for the
Feast of the
Circumcision.

THIRD MEDITATION

In the third meditation, now that your senses
have been purified, reflect on the glorious life
of the heavenly city of Jerusalem. Consider
the happiness, the joy, and the singing of the
multitude of angels and holy souls as they
attend God and receive from him their everlasting lustre in which they rejoice unceasingly.

My friend, you must ever yearn with all
your love and longing for this rejoicing, for
this fellowship, for this glory. Bewailing the
extension of your earthly misery, think, over
and again, of the nine different orders of
angels:* the archangels, angels, virtues; powers, principalities, dominations; thrones, cherubs and seraphs. Inasmuch as one may
compare a creature with the Creator, think
how this triple threesome directly attends
the highest Holy Trinity,[2] as its image and its
first and chief creation—full of life because
drawing directly from Life itself, wise because
drawing from Wisdom itself, unchanging by its
very Eternity, blessed from Blessedness itself,
and ever glorious because in the presence of
Eternity, Blessedness, and Glory. As Ezekiel
says [of them], 'You are stamped with the
seal of perfection, . . . of complete wisdom
and perfect beauty'; you are 'in Eden, the
garden of God'.* If you diligently consider
and ponder these words, they will inspire in
you an amazing and tender devotion toward
the holy angels. For, if such things could be
said about the fallen angels merely on account
of their creation, how much more empha-
tically must they be applied to the holy

*Cf. Col 1:16,
Eph 1:21, Bernard,
Csi 5.4-6 (SBOp 3:
470-77), John of
Damascus; FCh
37:205-210.*

Ezk 28:12.

angels who have given proof of their loyalty and preserved their innocence, the seal of their likeness to God.

As ministers of our salvation they are full of beauty, grace, and wisdom. They are 'ministering spirits' sent into the world to serve those who are to inherit salvation* in God's paradise with its secret delights, that is, with its unfathomable and everlasting joys which no eye has seen nor ear heard,† and everything else known to no one but to its recipient.* The first of the three orders exhibits the seal of likeness;* the second is full of beauty; the third shares the delights of God. More specifically, the thrones* are agents of God's saving deeds; the cherubs† have fullness of knowledge and understanding; and the seraphs* are aflame with consummate love.

*Heb 1:14. Cf.
Augustine, The
Trinity; FCh 45:
120-124 City of
God, Bks. 17-22
(FCh 24:140-149).

†1 Cor 2:9.

Rev 2:17.

Ezk 28:12.

*Cf. Bernard, Csi
5.11; SBOp 3:475;
CF 37:152-3.

†Ibid., (473, 475;
150-153).

*Ibid.

My friend, I do not want you to start investigating these things out of curiosity; rather, I want you to be affected by them sweetly and simply. After God and the blessed Virgin, put your trust in the help of those whom the loving Lord has made your helpers, your protectors, and fellow citizens. Recognize the mercy of the most loving Lord Who seizes every opportunity to promote your salvation.

God wished to bind his holy angels to us by a threefold ministry. First, seeing that God to whom they cleave loves us so greatly that he gave us his only-begotten Son, the Lord and creator of all, they incite us to love God. Thus they show that they truly love us. In this way they are *helpers*. Secondly, they are

Heb 1:14.

ministering spirits: they work on our salvation* and strengthen our faith. Thus they are
protectors. Thirdly, since the ruin of the
heavenly city, perpetrated by the fallen angels
and sinful man, has been repaired by Christ's
resurrection, they will present to God in the
general resurrection a glorious spouse, with-

Eph 5:27.

out stain in her body or wrinkles* in her soul.
Thus they are our fellow citizens.

Commend yourself daily to the holy angels
with full trust and devotion. Lead a holy,
prudent, and worthy life in their holy presence, for they unceasingly report your
thoughts and actions to God.

After the angels, think of the glory of the
holy patriarchs—of Abraham, Isaac, and Ja-

Rom 5:12.

cob, and all the rest—from whose seed* the
Lord Jesus came gloriously into the world
through the womb of the untouched Virgin.

Ps 102:5.

Consider the happy satiety* in the goods of
eternity; with it their long wait was fulfilled
by him whose day they longed for while on

Jn 8:56.

earth.* Admire their longanimity, their faith,
their patience, their obedience and hope;
admire how they believed in the promises,
how they obeyed the commandments, how
long-suffering they were in hope when they
put so much trust in the fulfillment of one
simple promise. Ask them with heed to make
you long with the same spirit and patience
for him who has already come and is present
in the sacraments of the Church.

Next turn to the stately number of proph-

Cf. Te Deum *hymn.*

ets* to whom God has spoken, revealing his
future designs. Illumined by the Holy Spirit,
they were able to see, as though they had

been present, events of the distant future: Christ's birth from the Virgin, his passion, resurrection, ascension, and whatever else he did on earth* consequent upon his incarnation for our salvation. They also foresaw the coming of the Holy Spirit, the judgment at the end of the world, and the glories of both the Church militant and the Church triumphant.

Ps 73:12.

Commend yourself to them in your prayers. Ask these experts in the knowledge of God, in strength of faith, in self-denial, constant meditation, and fervent devotion, these experts in obtaining God's mercy, to procure for you the grace of divine illumination that you may spurn the temporal world and develop a love and longing for eternal values.

Among the prophets pay particular honor to blessed John the Baptist who was conceived and announced by the same angel* who announced Christ and, though he had not yet been born, intimated the coming of Christ when, still enclosed in his mother's womb, he rejoiced in the visit of the Mother of the Lord. Of men born to women there were none greater than he.* He did not merely announce that Jesus would take away the sins of the world* but, seeing him, also pointed to him with his finger. He baptized the Son of God with his own hands and preceded Jesus into the nether world by his glorious martyrdom. Embrace him with a special love so that, by his holy intervention, he may share with you the spiritual joys he felt when meeting Christ and his blessed

Lk 1:26, 36.

Mt 11:11.

Jn 1:29.

Mother.

After this, pay honor to the council of the Apostles to whom the Lord gave the keys

Mt 16:18-19.

of the kingdom of heaven* and the seat of judgment. Unlike the patriarchs who saw him through signs or the prophets who saw him through mysteries, they saw God, as the prophet Isaiah says, eye to eye.* They

Is 52:8.

touched him with their hands, delighted in conversing with him, attended his councils, were with him at banquets. As one of them said, 'This is what we proclaim to you: what was from the beginning, what we have heard, what we have seen with our eyes and our hands have touched: we speak of the word of

1 Jn 1:1-2.

life'.*

Contemplate the happy conversation of those who have tasted his presence. Ponder the blessedness of that unique eagle who leaned on his Lord's breast during the [Last]

Jn 21:20.

Supper,* sipping from the sweet stream of

*Cf. Responsory,
II Nocturn, feast
of St John the
Evangelist,
27 December.

wisdom, the fountain of the Lord's breast.* How blessed are the twelve sitting in judgment,† on whose faith rests the Church

†Mt 19:28.

throughout the world. Seek their particular protection that, through their holy merits and intercession, they may secure for you the forgiveness of your sins in this life and eternal glory and an everlasting chair in the world to come.

Next, behold the purple-clad army of martyrs who washed and whitened their

Rev 22:14.
Eph 2:4.

robes in the blood of the Lamb.* In their exceeding love* they did not feel exterior flames, beatings, insults, crucifixions and all manner of contrived torments. Than they nobody had greater love; therefore, they now forever rejoice in blessed fruition in heaven. Humbly commend yourself to them, that through their example and holy intercession you may so imitate Christ's passion on earth that one day you will be united with them in the glory of heaven.

After this consider the glory of the saints. They cleansed their soul through holy confession, they cleansed their hands through good works; but, most importantly, they were purified through the sacred mysteries of the Body and Blood of Christ. Rejecting the delights of this world and fleeing secular praise, they bore a long martyrdom,[3] not by spilling their blood but by living a life of abnegation, solitude, silence, fasts, sparse clothing, harsh vigils, and uninterrupted penance. Because they ceaselessly practised all this, they earned this praise from the Church: 'They greatly excelled in combat . . . ' . *

Cf. the hymn, Jesu corona celsior, Lauds, Common of Confessors not bishops and Matins, feast of St Bernard, 20 August.

Seek, both by word and deed, the help of their holy prayers so that you may be able to join their company and receive the repose of eternal happiness for your temporal labors.

When recalling the saints, remember also that everyone will receive his reward on the basis of his own actions,* not those of some-else. Hence, if you wish to be with them in glory, do as they did. And, when thinking of the confessors, include the saintly hermits, the holy monks, and all who had been men of mercy in this world, for they are the sons of God who now stand as lords before the Lord of heaven and earth.*

1 Cor 3:8

Zc 4:14.

After this, pay honor to the choir of white-

Cf. the hymn,
Virginis proles opi-
fexque Matris,
*Matins, Common
of Virgins.*

Cf. Justinian, De
sanctimonialibus
vel viduis et de
successionibus
earum, *in* Codex
Theodosianus,
N. Maj. 6:1 and
6:3.

†Rev 14:4.

robed holy virgins who overcame their sex
and the world and, declining the luxury of
the world* and the temptations of our corruptible nature, preserved the chastity and
virginity of their body. They forsook the
bonds of marriage and renounced the blessing of children.* Firm in mind, action, and
love, they preferred to adhere to Christ
alone, their true Spouse who dwells in heaven.
Therefore, cleaving directly to him, they now
follow the Lamb wherever he goes,† chanting
that song of bodily integrity which none but
they may utter: 'O singular glory, O joy unspeakable: nothing can separate us from him
who is the joy of the angels, and the delight of
the blessed spirits anxious to gaze on him

1 P 1:12.

unceasingly'.* Labor without ceasing to bring
this about, to long for this majestic vision, so
that through the powerful intercession of the
holy virgins—and not your own merits—you
may attain chastity of soul and body in this
world and the garment of incorruption in the
world to come.

After you have cleared the battle-line of
your mind, consider next the glory and happiness of the heavenly city of Jerusalem. Consider, for instance, wherein consists the glory
of its saints, or how great is its joy where
Beauty itself reigns supreme, where dwells
Virtue, Power, Magnificence, Majesty and
Supreme Goodness—in a word, the triune

*Col 3:14.

God who is all in all,* who enlightens all
with knowledge and inflames all with love.
Here are all the holy angels, more glittering
than bright stars, and the patriarchs, rejoicing
in their victorious faith; here is the stately

group of jubilant prophets,* and the glorious choir of the Apostles. Here are the countless rows of martyrs who were victorious in combat and have received their crowns. Here are all the confessors rewarded for their fortitude, and the multitude of virgins crowned with lilies. Here are all the blessed who observed God's commandments and transformed their earthly assets into heavenly treasures.

Cf. Cyprian, De mortalitate; FCh 36:220.

How eagerly must we long for their happy and holy company! How severely must we censure ourselves for being sluggish, luke-warm, and obdurate in the very sight of such majesty! How we must blush that we did not fear their holy glances, but sinned before their very eyes and continue to do so up to this very day.

Confess your shortcomings, therefore, and say: 'Father, I have sinned against heaven and against you'.* I did not fear your holy angels and saints. I am not worthy to be called your son. Treat me, therefore, as one of your hired men so that, at least by fearing punishment and hoping for reward, I may stay away from sin and fear you, my Lord, as your servant, unworthy as I am to love you in the way a son does'.

Lk 15:18.

Prayer. All you angels, archangels, virtues, powers, principalities, dominations, thrones, cherubs, and seraphs, all you saints and elect of God who are fellow citizens of heaven and behold God directly in joyful contemplation, please keep me in your prayers so that the enemy may never deceive me* and that, through your intercession, my prayer may ascend to your holy temple where glory is

Ps 88:23.

given to God the Father, the Son, and the
Holy Spirit now and
for all ages to
come.
Amen.

NOTES TO A THREEFOLD EXERCISE

1. Cf. *The Register of Eudes of Rouen,* trans. S. M. Brown and J. F. O'Sullivan, Records of Civilization Series, vol. 72 (New York, 1964) 35 (on public penance).

2. Medieval writers seem to have been preoccupied with numbers and their meanings, symbolic, fantastic and otherwise. Probably its origin is to be found in Martianus Capella's *De nuptiis Philosophiae et Mercurii,* or Augustine, the most widely read author during the Middle Ages. His *De Trinitate* 5, Chapters 4-6, (FCh 45:139-144) are devoted to numbers and their meanings. Cf. *Christian Instruction,* trans. John J. Gavigan (FCh 4 [New York, 1947] 83-85) for further discussion on numbers. See also *Contra Faustum,* ch. 28.

3. On the concept of 'white martyrdom', see the letter of Sulpicius Severus to the Deacon Aurelius, trans. Bernard M. Peebles, FCh 7 (New York, 1949) 140-150. See also *Hymn Book of the Martyrs,* trans. M. Clement Eagan, FCh 43 (New York, 1962), for martyrs of all kinds. Origen's *Exhortation to Martyrdom,* trans. John J. O'Meara, ACW 19 (Westminster, 1956) is a treatise on 'white' as opposed to 'red' martyrdom. E. E. Malone, *The Monk and the Martyr* (Washington, 1950) 'traces only the general outlines of the historical development of the concept of spiritual martyrdom' (p. VIII).

A MIRROR
FOR NOVICES

A MIRROR FOR NOVICES

CHAPTER 1.
DAILY EXAMINATION
OF CONSCIENCE

WHEN YOU GO TO CONFESSION you may use words such as these,* adding or subtracting to what I am offering here in the measure you feel you have transgressed in these matters.

I think many idle thoughts and my mind wanders through such diverse places as castles, schools, gatherings; I dwell on them or take delight in them while I attend the Divine Office or when I should listen to the psalms or to spiritual reading. At times things I heard or saw in the past have come into my mind, distracting it, intentionally or unintentionally, from paying attention to the things of God. At times I have even conjured up in my heart matters I have neither seen nor heard. I spend my time on idle thoughts and do not realize it. (You must tell what kind of thoughts, to the extent you can remember; for instance:) I have thought long on building a church, writing books,* managing the house; or, on hunting, horse-racing, and other such things. At times the image of the coupling of man and woman comes to my mind; at other times my memory alone is occupied with such things. At times I take pleasure in them, at

Jb 42:3.
Cf. 2 Cor 5:13.

*Cf. Du Cange, Glossarium, 'facere literas'.

times I have feelings about them, at times I experience bodily sensations. At times I also consent to the desires of the body in food, drink, sleep* and other such things. At times I judge the words, the work, the efforts, the manners, the bearing and habit of others, either only in my heart or also by means of a gesture or words. I am anxious to learn about someone else's life but am indolent in learning about and negligent in correcting, my own life.

There are times when I complain about my handicaps, about my imaginary general ill-treatment by others, about the fasts, vigils, the coarse food, the hard and menial labor. I murmur about a harsh correction, about denied permissions, about an insult or injury I have received; or, when something is said, done or imposed on me against my will.

At times I extol myself on account of my handsome physique, my voice, my strength, my knowledge, my noble ancestry, my attire, my intelligent speech. I wish to be known and talked about, to be ahead of others in some matters. I take delight in these, and I think I am worth something when I am worth nothing.

At times I say, intentionally or unwittingly, words conducive to laughter.* At times I use unbecoming words, words of malice and detraction, of boasting or adulation, of hypocrisy or duplicity, speaking one way and feeling quite another toward someone else.*

At times I was angry, at other times disobedient. At times I do my own will; I delay going to prayer, to Mass, to the other

Cf. RB 49.

Cf. RB 6.

1 Kgs 22:20.

exercises, failing to give a good example to the others. I have no fear of expending precious time on trifles, on idleness and listlessness because both my fear of God and my good resolution are defective. At times I am quite unkind toward another in my mind, though this intent is not followed by action. At times I serve with less devotion, fear and reverence in God's presence when performing altar duties; I do the same in prayer and at work. And, I fear more the eyes of men than the eyes of God: at times I exert myself more on account of men than because of God.

I run more slowly to the Divine Office than to the table.* I bow absent-mindedly,[1] I obey unwillingly, and through many of my actions I show a low opinion of others and a high esteem of myself. I am a stumbling block to others by my bad example.

Cf. RB 43.

I do not keep my profession in the measure necessary or desirable. I do not recite the *debitum* [prayers prescribed for the dead]*, nor do I say the prescribed psalms and prayers with the proper intent for their designated beneficiaries.[2] Also, I have given things away or accepted things, and done this or that without permission or with an extorted permission.

See Guignard, 216, 169 (chapter).

Whatever I have knowingly or unwittingly done in these and all other matters against the will of God or against the Order, or whatever has been done by others because of me, whether I am aware of it or not, I confess my guilt before God: I promise amendment [of life] and ask for pardon.

This, then, is your mirror. To the extent
you feel yourself marred by these [faults], in
that measure confess [your guilt].

CHAPTER 2.
ON THE MANNER OF PRAYING:
PRAYER OF PETITION
AND THANKSGIVING

Prior to the prayer which should always follow confession, salute Mary, the mother of
the Lord, with the angel's prayer: 'Hail, holy,
glorious and ever-virgin Mary;'[3] do this up to
three times, with a genuflection if possible.
Next, give thanks to God for his countless
and immense blessings. Thank him for pro-
tecting you from all worldly dangers and
snares of the devil, also, for saving you from
the pains of hell by not allowing you to fall
into it, unlike many others who sinned [less
than you] and yet were punished more
severely than you for their sins. Give thanks
also for the religious vocation and the grace of
a pure heart; also, for the religious fervor and
holiness of your fellow monks among whom
he called you through his grace; and, for all
the favors he lavishes on the human race.

Beg the kindest Son of the Virgin for the
well-being of the whole world. As has been
given you from above, ask the Lord, either in
your heart alone or with unuttered requests
or with words of supplication, for forgiveness
and grace, for glory in the life to come, perseverance in your vocation, illumination of
your heart, for the loving pursuit of salvation,

and for those who are in any way distressed.

Then, bow low before the Lord or in honor of the Holy Trinity and say the antiphon 'We invoke you' and the collect 'Almighty and eternal God, you gave us . . . ' ,[4] genuflecting three times in honor of the Holy Trinity, or five times in honor of the five wounds of the crucified Lord. During this triple genuflection thank him that he predestined you from eternity out of so many thousands of reprobates, that he rescued you from countless evils and that out of an endless number of reprobates he has chosen you to a life of ineffable glory, happiness, dignity, and holiness; also, that he fashioned our nature in such greatness and loftiness, and mercifully restored it anew—and for other such things.

Next give thanks that God's majesty has held you in such high regard that he became a little boy, poor and weak, 'a worm not a man, the scorn of man despised by the people'.* Give thanks that he enlightened the world by his example and his teaching; that he sustained such a horrible and abject death; that by his resurrection he glorified our body, that by his ascension he raised it above all things; that he gave his most precious blood as a sweet pledge of his love;* that he left his gospel as a lasting testament; that he gave us countless models: the apostles, the martyrs, the confessors and virgins whose illustrious words, writings, miracles, passions, and deaths contributed to your salvation, to your comfort, to your prayer life, to your knowledge and life. Give thanks that all these cooperate unto your salvation.*

Ps 21:7

Gen 38:17.

**Rom 8:28.
See Amédée
Hallier, 'God
is Friendship: The
Key to Aelred of
Rievaulx' Christian Humanism',
28 (1967) 397-
403, for affectus.*

Thank God that directly after your birth he conferred on you the grace of baptism and the gift of salvation; also, that he rescued you from dangers, bore with you when you sinned, forgave you when you erred, and that he conferred on you the grace of continence, the hope of forgiveness, the grace of good works and the acceptance of suffering; for the measure of your suffering will determine the portion of your glory. Ask him, therefore, with all your heart, that he may increase his grace in you; that he may make you live worthily in his honor and for the salvation of your soul, and that he may prepare the joy of the saints for you and your fellow monks.

CHAPTER 3.
PREPARATION FOR
THE DIVINE OFFICE

The preparation of your heart [for the Divine Office] must extend to everything.

When it is time to get up for Matins, prepare yourself for worship. By that I mean you must jump up quickly from your bed and, once your drowsiness is dispelled, give thanks to divine mercy for having given you a good rest and the guardianship and protection of the angels. Next say for the dead, 'Rest eternal grant them, O Lord . . . ' . Then saluting the Mother of God, recite her Matins. The remaining hours of her Office you shall say in church when you have leisure and the available time.[5]

Arriving at the church, place your hand on

the door and say, 'Depart, evil thoughts, cares, intentions, affections of the heart and appetites of the body.* But you, my soul, enter into the joy of your Lord† that you may gaze on the loveliness of God and contemplate his holy temple.'* In front of the crucifix say, 'We adore you, O Christ, and we bless you because by your holy Cross you have redeemed the world.'*

When the opening words 'O God, come to my assistance' are intoned, pour out your heart like water in the presence of the Lord your God.* Say to yourself, 'Lord, I am weak, unable to open my mouth. Touch my mouth with your hand from on high,* and my soul will be filled with the riches of a banquet.* Then my mouth shall be filled with your praise, with your glory day by day.'*

Recite the verse said on your side of the choir, but say silently the verse of the other choir. Sprinkle each verse with the spice of spiritual meditation, for your soul is delicate and must be given choice foods.

As a general rule, focus your eyes on one place in front of you to the best of your ability and as your human frailty allows. Wandering eyes are most harmful to the mind's stability. To elicit humility, therefore, form a mental picture of the Lord as if he were lying in the manger in front of you. To feel compunction, visualize him suspended on the cross. Grieve and be thankful, because of the nails, the thorns, the spittle and the gaping wound in his side. Next move your eyes mentally all the way up to his divine heart, which houses all the treasures of his

Exordium Magnum 1.19, ed. Bruno Griesser (Rome, 1961) 72ff. Cf. PL 185:1015.
†Mt 25:21.

Ps 26:4.

Antiphon at Matins, Holy Cross Day, 14 September.

Lam 2:9.

Ps 143:7.
Ps 62:6.

Ps 70:8

Col 2:30.
wisdom and knowledge.* Then place your head between his shoulderblades and the cross and kiss the wounds which have mangled him so atrociously, and say to yourself

Mk 14:4.
Lk 15:17.
meanwhile, 'Why this waste* of Blood?' Here am I, perishing of thirst:* 'Why should I not come here, drink from the springs of the Saviour and cool my tongue?' Then listen to

Ps 84:9.
Jn 7:37.

Ps 33:9.
Heb 13:16.
what the Lord says within you:* 'He who is thirsty, let him come and drink'.* You will taste and see how good, how meek and humble of heart the Lord is.* Such efforts will obtain God's favor;* such intentions will draw him to you; such or similar affections will make Christ mentally present and he will not move on. The Lord will again reply 'What do you wish me to do for you?' as [he did] when the blind man cried out, 'Son of David,

Lk 18:38f.
Ps 41:5.
Lk 18:41.

Ps 105:5.
have mercy on me'.* O joyful shout of victory* which asked, 'What do you want me to do for you?'* Dear Jesus, my only wish is to be admitted among your chosen ones and to 'see the delights of your chosen one . . . ' .* Such thoughts will bring so much pleasure to your soul that even thinking about the angels will seem unattractive.[6]

I know a monk who quite often longed for the prolongation of Matins up to daylight.[7] This would allow him to think of the wonder-

*Ps 92:4.
†Cf. 2 Mac 1:7.

Ps 92:4.
ful waves,* of the violence and anguish† of Christ's suffering, that is, and of the power of the Lord on high,* that is, on the cross. He marveled at the great goodness of God the Creator and at the love of the Saviour who redeemed us with his precious blood. He also admired the great generosity of God who gives

us his grace beforehand* and has such great concern for the salvation of mankind.* He admired his great humility on the cross, his godliness as he died, his amazing power as he rose from the dead, and his glory as he ascended into heaven. He marveled at the mysteries of the cross, and the manner, the cause, and fruit of our redemption.

Ps 20:4.
Rev 5:9,
cf. Ps 102:4.

CHAPTER 4.
SEVEN WAYS OF MEDITATION

Look upon Jesus with wonderment and in like manner bless his holy name. Find out what is still lacking in your life with him. Ask this of him, in season and out of season; work on it constantly. Thank God for everything; thank him through Jesus.* As if you were a new-born child,* seek this kind of milk, that by it you may grow in health* until you wax feathered under the wings of the Mother of Grace.† Be content there and remain under the wings of such protection until [the time comes when] you are told, 'Go up higher,'* that is, rise to the more sublime and higher contemplation of God himself.

Col 3:17.
Quasimodo geniti infantes.
1 P 2:2.

†*An allusion to Aelred,* Spec car *1.5; PL:195:509D, 510A.*

Lk 14:10. Cf. William, Contemp 4; SCh 61bis:68-9; CF 3:40-42.*

FIRST WAY. Hear the words of *admiration:* 'O Lord, our Lord, how glorious is your name in all the earth.'* 'How great is your goodness, O Lord.'* 'Happy are they who dwell in your house.'* 'How lovely is your dwelling place.'* 'How great are your works.'† 'How sweet to my palate are your promises.'*

Ps 8:1f.
Ps 30:20.
Ps 83:5.
Ps 83:2.
†*Ps 91:6.*
Ps 118:103.

SECOND WAY. Hear the words of *praise.* For instance: 'Blessed be the name of the

Lord.'* 'Let all your works give you thanks.'†
'May all flesh bless his holy name.'*

THIRD WAY. Making *comparisons*. For
instance, 'As a father has compassion on his
children.'* 'As the hind longs for the running
waters.'* 'My soul thirsts for you like
parched land.'* 'As with the riches of a banquet shall my soul be satisfied.'* Reflecting
on human frailty one should say, 'We are
dust.'* 'Man's days are like those of grass.'†
'May they be like grass on the housetops,'*
and the like.

FOURTH WAY. The voice of *longing*. For
instance: 'When shall I go and behold the face
of God.'* The voice of longing and clamoring
also says: 'Awake! Why are you asleep,
O Lord? Why do you hide your face?'*
'Why do you forget me?'* and the like.

FIFTH WAY. Form a mental picture of
Jesus walking through the choir, followed by
angels carrying twelve baskets of fragments*
which have fallen from their masters' tables*
in that heavenly court which God has prepared for those who love him* and which he
in his goodness has provided for the needy,*
and say: 'There is no bread in my house'.*
Also, 'Withered and dried up like grass is my
heart; I forget to eat my bread'.* Then, the
source of mercy will say to you, 'Open wide
your mouth and I will fill it'.*

SIXTH WAY. Having received God's blessing and partaken of his manna, let all your
bones rejoice in the Lord and say, 'O Lord,
who is like you?'* Do this in order to subsist
on this nourishment for forty nights and
forty days* and to feel all the while how true

*Ps 112:2.
†Ps 144:10.
*Ps 144:21.

Ps 102:13.
Ps 41:2.
Ps 142:6.
Ps 62:6.

*Ps 102:14.
†Ps 102:15.
*Ps 128:6.

Ps 41:3.

Ps 43:23f.
Ps 41:10.

Mt 14:20.
Mt 15:27.

1 Cor 2:9.
Ps 67:11.
Is 3:7.

Ps 101:5.

Ps 80:11.

Ps 34:10.

1 K 19:8.

it is that 'those who seek the Lord lack no
good thing.'*   *Ps 33:11.*

SEVENTH WAY. You must always give
thanks in your heart and with your lips.
Thank God, above all, that he has saved you
from many dangers and from the snares of
the hunters,* especially in such matters as   *Ps 90:3.*
allurements of the flesh and of the world,
suggested by the devil.

CHAPTER 5.
SUMMARY

Wherever you are, use these high-sounding
cymbals:* Adore God's goodness by using   *Ps 150:5.*
as instruments what you see and hear. At
other times, bless him so that you may be
filled with his blessings. At still other times,
long and sigh for the glory of his coun-
tenance.* In this way you will stir up God's   *2 Cor 3:7.*
grace within you.

Moreover, do not hesitate to give form in
your heart to anything that can be activated
in you by God or the angels, or that can be
said or that can happen in conjunction with
the various events and circumstances of our
Redemption.

In every instance, render incessant thanks
to God.

CHAPTER 6.
VARIOUS FORMS OF MEDITATION

In formulating subjects for meditation, bring

*Cf. Aelred, Ann 8
(PL 195:254C);
Amadeus, Hom 3
(SCh 72:102-8;
CF 18:84-6).

*Cf. Bernard, Miss
3.1-2,4.8; SBOp
2:34,37,40; CF 18:
33-5,53-4.

Jn 20:30.

*Inst incl; PL 32:
1451-74; SCh 76;
CF 2.

*Lk 2:34f.
†Lk 2:46.

*Cf. Aelred, Jesu
6-7 (PL 194:853f.;
SCh 60:83-91;
CF 2:9-13), Ama-
deus, Hom 1 (SCh
72:58-62; CF 18:
62-3), Isaac, 1 Epi
14 (SCh 130:
188-90; CF 11:
57-62).
*Cf. Amadeus,
Hom 6 (SCh 72:
171-3; CF 18:110),
William, Contemp
10 (SCh 61bis: 92;
CF 3:51-3).
†Lk 4:2, cf. Mt 4:
2, Mk 1:13.
**Pr 8:31.

to mind the events of salvation history. In thinking of the angel saluting Mary, imagine reverently that the blessed Mary was reading the Prophet Isaiah when she was saluted by the angel;* also, that she experienced unspeakable joy when she received the fullness of grace; that she realized power was bestowed upon her over heaven and earth, the sea and all its depths, and, that on her nod of assent hung the salvation of the world and the reopening of heaven.*

Next, dwell much on the birth of Christ, also on things not written down [in the Gospels]:* for instance, how he appeared to the Magi or what his facial expression was like that it caused these important and powerful men to offer gifts in humble prostration. What I have glossed over here, briefly and succinctly, you will find in more detail in Aelred's *Meditations* which he wrote in his short treatise entitled, *A Rule of Life for a Recluse.*

Recalling the Presentation in the temple, see how Simeon was filled with the Holy Spirit.* Recall the three-day search† during which Joseph and Mary sought him everywhere. Where was he in the meantime? Was he begging from door to door? Was he amidst the angels during these three days?*

Think also of his baptism and how intently the onlookers fixed their gaze on this revelation of his majesty.* Think of his fast in the desert for forty days† and what solitude he sustained, he who delights to be with the sons of men.** Look back upon his preaching activity when all were amazed about the words of grace which proceeded from his mouth.* Recall how all rejoiced about his favors and glorious deeds* as he healed the sick or spent the nights in prayer, or, in his weariness, sat on the wall of the water well* and, after asking the woman humbly and soothingly for water, the fountain of life promised her life everlasting in return.* Think of his tenderness in receiving Mary Magdalen when, in tears,* he proceeded to raise Lazarus from the dead.

Retrace the procession in Jerusalem when the Lord of Lords, seated on an ass* which was without saddle, without bit, without bridle, hastened toward the cross. Call to mind the washing of the feet;* what an amazing sight it was to see God at the feet of fishermen, of a tax collector and of others like them. See him mentally as he prayed at the time of his betrayal; recall his great weariness, fear, and sadness, and the long drawn-out agony while he was absorbed in prayer; and how the situation changed when Judas kissed him; how he was arrested by the mob while the apostles deserted him.*

Recall his Passion in like manner: the derision, spitting, cuffing, chaining of his hands, blindfolding, the scourging ordered by Pilate, the mockery of Herod, the jeering voices which demanded his crucifixion and the mocking soldiers intoxicated with sour wine who genuflected before him and hit him on the head with rods. See him on the cross, his hands elevated 'like the evening sacrifice'*— his limbs stretched, his face pale, his bones in pain, his joints broken—and his great bitterness

Lk 4:22.

Lk 9:43, 14:4, 22:51, Mt 21:14.

Jn 4:6-26.

Jn 4:14.
Jn 11:35.

Mt 21:2-7.

Jn 12:4, 13:1-11.

Mk 14:50.

Ps 140:2.

Heb 4:12.

which finally brought on the separation of his
soul and spirit.*

Ps 103:25.

I firmly believe that, if you diligently cultivate these or similar thoughts as time permits,
you will find a sea 'great and wide'.*

Picture Jesus on the cross, heaped with
reproaches and derision, his body completely
lacerated, his flesh torn by whips and thorns
as he hung nailed to the cross. Visualize him
as he directs his merciful and loving eyes on

*Jn 17:12. See
Augustine,
Enchiridion 27;
PL 40:245.

you, the son of perdition.* Filled with grief,
cast aside your ingratitude and rebuke your
hardness of heart.

Realize who is suffering. See what he is
going through and for whom, how dearly he
has purchased your love, how willingly he
gave himself for you; there the weakness of
hanging there will be yours, the pallor of
shaking limbs yours, the shedding of blood
yours, and the last breath of the crucified
yours.

When thinking of Christ's burial, bring to
mind the insensibility of his dying limbs, the
violence of his accusers, the seeping of his
wounds; also, the solicitude of his disciples

*William, Cant;
SCh 82:198;
CF 6:68.

who anointed, wrapped, and buried him,*
and the close watch kept by the soldiers. I believe that you too will weep if you give serious
thought to these. Ask, therefore: where then
was the heart of God and, above all, the
power of God in whose 'hands are the depths

Ps 94:4.

of the earth'?*

Call to mind Christ's descent into hell.
Imagine the stupefaction he inflicted on the
devils who were ready for a feast, as the
brightness of the new light shone on them;

imagine the silence he imposed on their wailing and gnashing of teeth. Visualize the hope he infused in the elect who were sitting in darkness and the shadow of death,* when he snatched them from the hand of the enemy, from the very throat of the devil, from the depths of hell as he recalled them to his own wonderful light.*

Lk 1:79.

*Cf. Amadeus, Hom 6; SCh 72: 163-4; CF 18:111.

Thinking of the resurrection, bring to mind how great was the light emanating from Christ's body, the joy of the disciples, the congratulation offered to his Mother the Virgin Mary, though one would be right in thinking that it was not adequate in view of her overwhelming joy.* Think of the great interest of those who touched his wounds, who thrust their hands into his most precious side and sighed at each puncture in his head, made by the points of the thorns.

Cf. ibid. (161; 109), Baldwin, Sacr (SCh 93:183-7).

If you concentrate on all this, I am certain you will almost be breathless in admiration, unable to say anything but 'My Lord and my God'.*

Jn 20:28.

Recalling his ascension, be mindful of the following: if you hasten for his holy blessing, he, with his hands raised, will bless you together with the apostles. If like them you follow, in desire and with tears, the ascending Lord, if with all the others, you yearn to meet and contemplate him, to the admiration of the attending host you will be admitted to the perfectly harmonious heavenly choirs who follow the Lord Jesus Christ unto the interior veils,* unto the very presence of God the Father. 'As wax melts before the fire,'* as a pile of silver is rendered soft by

Heb 6:19.

Ps 67:3.

Pr 27:11.   heat,* so will your affections overflow your
Ps 72:7.   heart.* Yearning and pining for the courts of
Ps 83:3.   the Lord,* you will ascend to God with your
                   whole heart; your whole being will be drawn
                   to him; you will be united to him with all
                   your strength. You will become one with
1 Cor 6:17   him* for all eternity.

                   Whenever you consider these events and
                   feel that you had, so to say, actually been
                   present at each, you will be lifted up in won-
                   derment and gratitude. If you make use of the
                   other things mentioned above, you will dis-
                   cover what the psalmist had in mind when he
                   said, 'The thoughts of men shall recall your
Ps 75:11.   glorious deeds'.*

CHAPTER 7.
DAILY MEDITATION ON ALL THE
PRECEDING NOT NECESSARY

                   Bear in mind that these themes must not be
                   pondered every day of the week, nor are all to
Ps 32:2.   be meditated on simultaneously. Pluck* now
                   this, now that of the above-mentioned nine-
                   teen chords: the angel's salutation to Mary,
                   the birth of Our Lord, and all the rest. You
Sir 40:21.   will produce a sweet melody* in the Lord's
                   ear if you add, with frequent interchanges and
                   in a voice of exultation and praise, the seven
                   modes or tones of admiration, praise, com-
                   passion, longing, hunger, feeding, and thanks-
                   giving. With such fare you will also gladden
Ps 45:5.   the entire City of God.*

                   On the way out of the choir say, 'Lord,
                   I still have psalms, hymns, and prayers to say

in private. "Your statutes are the theme of
my song in the place of my exile."* Leaving   *Ps 118:54*
public prayer behind me, I will continue to
sing your praise* and voice my thanks as I go   *Ps 107:2.*
about in your house.'*   *Ps 26:6.*

CHAPTER 8.
TIME SUITABLE FOR
MEDITATION

It is the will of God that we meditate at all
times* and let no hour pass without making   *Ps 118:15; 118:77;*
spiritual progress; however, a definite time   *118:174.*
should be set aside when we are more fully
alone with God. According to Jerome, the
morning, that is, the time between dawn and
the third hour, is best suited to this.[8]

CHAPTER 9.
ATTEND MASS GLADLY

When it is time for Mass, accept the invitation
to attend private Masses as you would if you
were to see the bread of angels falling to you
from heaven.* Imagine that you want to take   *Cf. Baldwin, Sacr;*
it and keep it for yourself, but that someone   *SCh 93:268-70,*
is trying to snatch that piece of bread[9] from   *SCh 94:337-41.*
your very throat while you are starving.

CHAPTER 10.
PREPARATION FOR CHAPTER

In the Chapter Room,[10] put on the armor

of God with diligence:* the helmet of provi-
dence, the breast-plate of patience,* and the
shield of mercy. Use them to dispose of both
just and undeserved accusations. In case you
have transgressed say only, 'I will make
amends'. If you have not transgressed, say, 'I
do not remember. I will make amends.' Do
not add to or subtract anything from these
words or let anything further be wrenched
from you by way of accusations of beatings.

THE CHAPTER PRECEDING
OUR LORD'S PASSION

When you step forward for judgment, think
of Christ's trial before the Praetor Pilate when
the Pharisees acted as his accusers and the
soldiers flogged him, all without legitimate
cause. Think of the trials of the holy martyrs
as they stood before kings and judges presiding
with their staffs. Think of your own death
and harsh trial before God when thousands
of devils will shout accusations against you
and a million of them will bear false witness
against you.

   If you are being dealt with harshly, you
will be soothed if you do the following: think
of your accuser as the razor of God who
wishes to remove your unsightly hair so that
you will appear fairer in beauty than the

sons of men* and be more pleasing in the
presence of God in the light of the living;*
and that the King on whom the angels desire
to gaze* desires your beauty. Think that this
correction is an extra pittance sent to you

from heaven. It is not always spiced with
cinnamon, but it still delights even when
seasoned with mustard. If at all possible, re-
compense your accuser, whoever he may be,
on that same day with some favor, for the
simple reason that his intent was to free
you from the deformity of sin.

CHAPTER 11.
WORK

When you go to work, do what has to be done
in such a way that your concern for the task
at hand will not divert your mind from the
things of God.

During the rest period, do not look for a
secluded corner or sit apart from the others;
rather, let your eyes be upon the faithful.*   *Ps 100:6.*
Sit with Jesus in the midst of the learned*   *Lk 2:46.*
and quietly think about your eternal rest.

One of our brothers, sitting alone and
apart from the others during the rest period,
began to be gravely beset by temptations of
the flesh; he heard a voice saying to him,
'Go down to the camp'.* When he joined the   *Jdg 7:9f.*
others, the temptation ceased.

CHAPTER 12.
MEALS

When you go to the refectory, be neither the
first nor the last to enter. When you cannot
eat the food set before you, do not allow it to
be changed at all; instead, eat a little in order

to give the impression of having eaten. If someone insists that you eat, answer only with the sign, 'It's good; it's plentiful; it's gone'. Think of how many worked to prepare your food, and especially how diligently the Lord supplies you with spiritual delights by way of learned teachers. Think of the countless dangers endured by seamen in order to provide fish to satisfy the wants of your flesh and thank God for each bite.[11] Think also of the crucified Christ in the church, waiting for you to come and thank him. And think of Christ, standing in the cold at the door, waiting for what you have left over.

Make a cross from five bread crumbs and say to yourself, 'Here the feet, there the hands were nailed to the cross; here the head rested, there through his side flowed, in a mixture of blood and water, his mercy and plenteous redemption'.* Occasionally put aside one third of the extra portion of food, or of your pound of bread, and say, 'Lord, what will you give me for this portion? Let's strike a bargain. What will you give me by way of tears, holy desires, consolations of the Holy Spirit, protections of your saving grace,* the look of your most loving eyes for this piece of bread?'

Ps 129:7.

Ps 17:36.

CHAPTER 13.
ABSTINENCE

I absolutely forbid total abstinence. You are to eat each day the following measure of food: while you are growing, eat three-fourths

of your pound of bread;[12] put aside the
fourth part. Later on, two parts will be
enough after you divided the loaf into three
portions. Of the two cooked vegetable dishes*   *RB 39.*
which are easily absorbed and digested, take
one if it is good or half a portion from each
of the two dishes if both seem good to you. If
the measure of wine or beer placed before you
is medium-sized or small, take three-fourths
or almost all, for the better digestion of your
food and for avoiding headache. But forever
be careful not to exceed the bounds of sobri-
ety, mindful of Holy Scripture's warning of
the great evils which befell Noah, Lot, and
Nabal from intoxication.* Seek particularly   *Gen 9:20; 19:30;*
that kind of abstinence which is recom-   *1 Sam 25:36, 39.*
mended by the Apostle, who managed to be
content with what he had.* Always be con-   *Heb 13:5.*
tent with and thankful for whatever is set
before you. No matter what is provided for
you, be it in abundance or otherwise, always
bless God and never complain.

CHAPTER 14.
NOCTURNAL EMISSION[13]

Should you happen to have a nocturnal emis-
sion while sleeping, do not be too upset about
it. But if you should be invited to serve at a
private Mass, be sure to make a sign in the
presence of the brethren and humbly excuse
yourself, as is our custom, so that everybody
will know about your defilement during the
night. One of us did this also in the presence
of the novices and even when no one called

him to serve, so that he would be more
ashamed; he was so freed from temptation
that he seldom experienced or felt such
prurient desires more than once or twice a
year. This shows how true is God's word, 'I
will honor those who honor me';* and, 'He
who humbles himself shall be exalted';* and,
'God bestows his favor on the lowly'.*

1 Sam 2:30.

Lk 14:11.

Jm 4:6.

CHAPTER 15.
READING
THE SACRED SCRIPTURES

**See Guignard,
Les monuments
primitifs, 85-287.*

**Vitae patrum;
PL 73-74. Cf. Ael-
red, Inst incl (SCh
76:67; CF 2:56).*

During the time for reading,* you as a
beginner must be careful to read only our
own Book of Usages, our Antiphonary, the
Lives of the Fathers* and the *Dialogues*
of blessed Gregory.[14] Later on, when you
have matured in the religious life and become
more experienced in spiritual exercises, add
more solid food, depending on the time and
place, each year by studying the Old and New
Testaments.

Do not read the Holy Scriptures[15] for the
purpose of acquiring knowledge, because that
is merely curiosity, or that you may become
known and be given empty recognition, because that is vanity; nor should you read them
in order to find material with which to rail
against those whom you dislike, because that

*Bernard, SC 36.3;
SBOp 2:3-4;
CF 7:176.*

is evil.* Instead, employ the Scriptures as
a substitute for a mirror wherein the soul
somehow finds a reflection of its own image.
It sees there things that are corrupt and cor-
rects them; and things that are beautiful

which contribute to its radiance. Bear in mind that the words you are reading are the words of God who decreed that his law not only be known and read, but also fulfilled and implemented. 'Prudent are' therefore 'all who live by it.'* Also, try to memorize what you have read.†[15]

A certain monk who had no understanding of the Scriptures but was a good and simple man decided, by the inspiration of the Holy Spirit, to dedicate the first verse of the psalmody to the Father, the second to the Son, and the third to the Holy Spirit. He went on to do the same with all the other verses. Completely occupied with the application of the psalm verses, he reached such purity of heart that he cured those possessed by the devil.

*Ps 110:10. Cf. Bernard, ibid.
†Aelred, Inst incl 20; SCh 76:95; CF 2:68.*

CHAPTER 16.
BOOKS TO BE PARTICULARLY STUDIED

The writings of our father Benedict,* the *Confessions* of Augustine,† his *Commentaries on the Psalter*,** especially on Psalms 30-109 and 119-150. Gilbert's [*Sermons*] *on the Song of Songs** has been written, so to say, for your particular needs. It is good for your soul, it enriches your spirit and instructs your mind with the fat of a more perfect charity. Read, therefore, and cherish these writings before anything else.

Read also the *Conferences* of John Cassian,* the *Letters* of blessed Jerome dealing

*The Rule of St Benedict.
†PL 32:659-868. Cf. Aelred, Inst incl; SCh 76:27-28.
**Enarrationes in Psalmos, 30-109; 119-150; PL 36: 226; 37:1445, 1596-1966.*

of Hoyland, PL 184:11-252; CF 14,20,26.

PL 49:447-1328; Jean Cassien, Conférences, ed. J. C. Guy, SCh 42,54, 64 (Paris, 1955-1959).

PL 184:307-354;
CF 12.

with the lives of the monks or written in praise of the eremitical life,[16] the writings of Aelred,[17] [the letter] of William of Saint Thierry to the Brothers of Mont–Dieu,* and other instructive and illuminative writings on the spiritual life. However, they must be chosen and read with discretion and not a little caution so that they will teach you modesty in behavior, a knowledge of the virtues, experience in the exercise of good works, and perseverance in the religious life you have embraced.

Tob 14:4.

Let me conclude in summary: from all your readings strive to make progress in virtue.* Never cast aside or change your monastic profession once you have made your choice. As John Cassian said, 'You may pick the flowers from the field over which you walk, but you are not to pick the field itself.'* Keep also, and pursue as a labor of love the commendable instruction given to the Brothers of Mont–Dieu: 'Deposit a portion of the daily reading in the depths of your memory. There it is better digested and more abundantly ruminated upon on recall.'* Meditate on it gladly and at length.**

*Not Cassian, but
a paraphrase of a
sentence in Jer-
ome's Letter 130
to Demetriadis,
PL 22:1115.

*For the meaning
of "ruminating" on
the Scriptures in
Pachomian monas-
teries, see Veilleux,
La liturgie, supra
n. 149, pp. 267-
278.

**1 Tim 4:15.

Banish altogether the arguments of quibblers and the disputations of wranglers, be they found in secular or spiritual books, if you consider me your friend, for they disturb the tranquility and serenity of your mind and on occasion completely destroy it.

CHAPTER 17.
PRIVATE MEDITATION

After returning your book spend some time in
private meditation. Do this wherever you find
a place suitable for such a purpose, that is,
wherever you encounter God's goodness. Say
at the outset, 'What shall I return to the Lord
for all he has given to me?'* This is the first
and greatest question. The second question is
like the first one: 'My soul, what is your debt
to the Lord?'* Then, calling upon the angels,
say, 'Come and listen, all you who fear God,
and I will tell you the great things he has done
for me.'* Next, turn your eyes in affection
toward God and say, 'O Lord, great indeed is
your mercy towards me'.* Tell him, therefore, 'Show me, O Lord, where you eat,
where you lie at mid-day',* and ask, 'Rabbi,
where do you dwell?,'* 'O Lord, where are
you going?,'* and, 'Why can I not follow
you?'

If an evil thought should intrude while your
heart is moved and beating like this at the
gates of paradise, react at once and say,
'Whose image and inscription is this?'* On
hearing that it is Caesar's, the prince of this
world, that is, the devil's, put an end to it and
say, 'Most wicked one, keep your money for
yourself and perish with it.* Get out of my
sight, Satan.† The door is already closed and
the Lord is eating his Pasch here.** I am too
busy to open it for you.'

These things seem senseless and frivolous
only to fools, but not to him who meditated
and prayed day and night, thus detaining

Ps 115:12.

Mt 22:36.

Ps 65:16.

Ps 85:13.

Sg 1:6f.
Jn 1:38.
Jn 13:36-37.

Mt 22:20

Ac 8:20.

†*Mk 8:33. Cf. Ael-
red, Inst incl 16:
SCh 76:209-11;
CF 2:65-6.*

**Lk 11:7.*

the devil over a ten day period so that he could not move on.

Should an evil thought persist, counteract it by making the sign of the cross.

CHAPTER 18.
THE POWER OF
THE SIGN OF THE CROSS

A nun in this area held the sign of the holy cross in such great reverence that as she was being carried to her grave the face of the crucified Christ turned around toward her, in the direction she was being carried. Thus, contrary to what is usual, the head of the cross remained steadfast in that position, turned-around and looking toward her. Another nun related to someone that her body putrified but her thumb did not because with it she was wont to make the sign of the cross.

Say private prayers twice each day; go to confession twice each week. Beware, lest in contact with or by consent of another, you do or allow anything to be done to you for which

Ps 68:8, Jer 31:19. you should feel shame or bear reproach.* Do not flee from or seek private or public conversation, but remember that they are wild fruit grown in the woods. Remember also what has been written: 'Every word which does not edify the listener becomes a danger

Cf. Imitatio   to him who speaks it';* and what the Apostle
Christi, *10:2.*   said: 'Never let evil talk pass your lips; say
                    only the good things men need to hear, things
Eph 4:29.   that will really help them'.*

CHAPTER 19.
AVOID BOASTING

I warn you that there are two matters which you should particularly avoid. Insofar as it is within your power, let nobody know about your good efforts lest you incur the vice of hidden pride or of being puffed up [with your own importance]. Also, do not think it is safe to dwell on them as often as you want to.

When you see someone else fervent in prayer, silence, patience, obedience, and other such exercises, give thanks to God that he has sent you such an example and do not be envious. When you see that another is troubled, give thanks to God that that cloud is not passing over you and say, 'What effect would that temptation have on me if God permitted it?'* Do not pass judgment on another's shortcomings or pierce the walls of his conscience, but think of what happens to housebreakers these days. *Sir 34:9.*

When you approach the prior to request something, always be prepared for a refusal. If this happens, say to yourself: 'What is more suited to a little donkey than a bridle and goad? I thank you, Lord, for this refusal; for this is how you build up strength within me.* I can lay claim to almost nothing in this monastery beyond the ashes of penance, a hair cloth, and a crucifix.' *Ps 137:3.*

CHAPTER 20.
MEDITATION WHEN YOU
GO TO BED

Be sure to keep the following in mind when you are going to bed. Look at your coarse woollen blanket and bedcovers and compare your bed to your grave, just as if you were entering it for burial. In bed, commend your body and soul into those blessed hands which for your sake were nailed to the cross. Beg the Lord of all the saints to look upon you with mercy, to protect you from sin and dangers, to send from heaven his holy angels to guard you, to comfort you and fortify you in the attainment of what is good. Beg him also to give refreshment to all the faithful departed so that, safe and unharmed, they may attain his mercy and forever enjoy his protection. Thereafter, supplicate the blessed Mary, saying, 'Hail, holy, glorious, and perpetual Virgin, full of grace . . . ' . Then add the prayer, 'May the souls of all the faithful departed through the mercy of God rest in peace. Amen.'* If you can sleep, all is well; if you cannot, experience has proved that if you say the Athanasian Creed* seven times or the Seven Penitential Psalms,** you will fall asleep.

From the Office of the Dead.

The Symbol, said at Prime on Sunday.

**Ps 6,31,37,50, 101,129,142.*

CHAPTER 21.
AVOID UNNECESSARY DISPLAY

Keep to yourself all efforts of this kind. Present yourself to all as humble, peaceful, agreeable, and zealous in the performance of your duties. Disguise your private meditations to the best of your ability. In the performance of your public and private exercises, have concern for what is profitable for others, but do so without unnecessary display on your part.

CHAPTER 22.
THE VALUE OF OBEDIENCE

Above and beyond everything else, be prepared to obey with an alert mind and agreeable face.* That you may understand the efficacy and good of this virtue, think of the monk Gerard. When Gerard had almost despaired of God's mercy, his abbot pledged himself as surety that he would not perish for the greatness of his sins if he would continue in obedience to the abbot's commands and remain in the Order. As he was dying, he lay with his eyes closed and his mind absent.* When his abbot visited him on the third day, Gerard opened his eyes and said, 'Obedience is good. I have been to Christ's judgment seat and saw him face to face. He said to me, "Here is your place among your brothers; no monk of your Order will perish if he loves his Order. He is cleansed either at the moment of death or shortly thereafter".' After he had said this, he received Holy Communion and died.[18]

Exhortation. Well done, good brother, remain in the Lord. Fulfill my joy, refresh my soul.*

Cf. RB 71.

In mentis excessus: Ps 67:28.

Ph 1:20.

What I am writing here is not for the many,
but for you alone. As someone or other once
said, 'We are treasure enough for each other'.*

Source unknown.

CHAPTER 23.
MEDITATION DAY AND NIGHT

When going to bed, think of Christ's burial
and your own. When it comes time to rise,
think of the resurrection. During psalmody
[Matins] think of the angels' joy.* At Lauds,
think of the apprehended Christ. At Prime,
think of Christ standing before Pilate, bound
to a pillar, manhandled harshly and flogged
most severely. During Terce, think of Christ
raised on the cross or ascending into heaven,
and of the descent of the Holy Spirit on the
Apostles. At Sext, think of the darkness which
fell on the earth up to the ninth hour.* Embrace Christ's knees or make for yourself a
headrest* from the nails in his feet, all the
while admiring his unutterable poverty* because, as †Bernard said, 'He had no earth for
his foot, no drink for his mouth, no wood to
lay his head on, no covering for his side, no
friend to console him'. Or, if you wish,
murmur such other words as, 'Remember me,
O Lord, when you come into your kingdom'.* At None, think of Christ dying and
say, 'Clearly, this was the Son of God'.*
Then, link yourself to his soul as he goes
down into hell. Together with him, liberate
those who are fettered in hell; thrust the devil
back into the very depths of hell. At Vespers,
run back to the Lord's cross and, with Joseph

*Cf. Aelred, Inst
incl 9-10; SCh 76:
64-8; CF 2:55-7.
Compare Stephen's
thoughts on the
Office with Aelred's
in La Vie de Re-
cluse, pp. 65-69.

Mt 27:45.

Ezk 13:18.

*Cf. Gilbert, SC
2.1; PL 184:210;
CF 14:55.
†Pseudo-Bernard.

Lk 23:42.
Mt 27:54.*

and Nicodemus, be completely filled with
anxiety. Ask that Christ be laid away with all
tenderness and calm. When arriving for Compline, think how you are going to bed and yet
watching the Lord's tomb so that when he
arises you can run and, with Mary Magdalen,[19] hold his feet.

CHAPTER 24.
REMEDIES AGAINST
TEMPTATIONS

Learn to apply a remedy against the vices
which seek to assert themselves. When de-
pressed and lukewarm, remember that you
may be allowed to work today but perhaps
not tomorrow,* for you do not know what   *Is 22:13.*
the next day may bring.* When you throb   *Pr 27:1.*
with passion, counteract it by thinking of the
eternal fire. When you are tempted to disobedience, think that disobedience is apos-
tasy; as the Book of Kings says, 'The refusal
to obey is like the crime of idolatry'.* When   *1 Sam 15:23.*
you are plagued by impatience, think of what
Christ bore for your sake. When vainglory pul-
sates within you, think that that of which
you are boasting is not yours and that you
will have to pay the interest. When tempted
by pride, think of your models. When your
will urges you in the direction of evil, remember that man will be judged even for mere
intention or attachment to an act, though
he will be condemned for the act itself or the
fatal word; and that he will be far more
gravely punished the greater his progress in

perversity of will and the more serious the sin.

When you are tempted to do the bare minimum, remember: In what measure you mete shall it be measured to you in return.* When you have to put up with a loss, remember that you brought nothing into this world and will take nothing out of it.* When you are afflicted, remember that the sufferings of this world cannot be compared with our future glory.* When you are elated with the pride of having done good, remember how many good things you have failed to do, and the more you hide your good deeds now, the more resplendent you will be at the judgment. When affluence gives way to aridity, remember the verse, 'A moment's affliction must not bring forgetfulness of past delights'.*

When you are given high praise, remember that it is like the wind which inflates. When you feel happy about your body and your strength, remember how quickly they can be taken away by the smallest fever. When your mind is puffed up with knowledge, remember that your knowledge of yourself is not yet perfect and that much remains hidden from you according to that saying, 'You were blind when even a child could see it'. When you feel an inordinate urge for good food and drink or clothes, answer a fool according to his folly,* that is, say to your corruptible body that it is destined to become a heap of dirt and food for worms.* When the weight of [monastic] observances and the rigors of its discipline vex you, think of what St Jerome said, 'No work is hard, no time is long if it secures eternal

Mt 7:2.

Cf. 1 Tm 6:7.

Rom 8:18.

Qo 11:27.

Pr 26:5.

1 Mac 2:62. Cf. Zeph 1:17, Jb 25:6; Ps 21:7.

glory'.[20] And when you probe your thoughts, never think that you are doing pretty well but that you are still lacking in perfection.*

1 Mac 13:5.
Cf. Num 6:21.

When a desire to ride horseback plagues you remember what happened to Dinah who had only gone outside to take a walk.* If you feel that by your going out some good will happen to your monastery, remember Esau's departure; while busily hunting, he lost his father's blessing.* If you have a strong desire to visit your parents, remember Tamar, David's daughter, who, even though she had her father's permission to leave her chamber to visit her sick brother, was corrupted by him.*

Gen 34:1

Gen 27:1-46.

2 Sam 13:1-14.

Dear son, I am warning you that of all the snares of the ancient enemy you must avoid the following as you would avoid the noonday devil: from the time you entered religion never entertain, cherish, or give credence to the suggestion that it is of scant use to you to remain, that you could be more useful to yourself and others in another way of life, another habit. For, if you incline your ear* and heart to these kinds of thoughts, they will so divide and distract your mind that it will not be able to retain the good advice of your master or any unction of grace or the seasoning of spiritual flavor. Your heart will become like a broken jar which will not hold wisdom. Your mind will be torn apart trying to choose between many professions and pursuits. The consequence will be the danger that not only weariness but a frightful despondency over the good work you have begun will overwhelm you.

Ps 16:6.

Abbot Nestor spoke pointedly on this subject when he said in his Conferences: 'When fickle and ill-grounded minds hear others commended for their virtues and for their zeal, they are so set ablaze by the praise that they immediately wish to embrace their example and discipline; but in vain. Such change and divergence from their own way of life reaps them a loss and not a gain because he who follows after many things will not attain anything completely. Thus, it is expedient to each that, according to the path which he has chosen and the grace he has received, he strive with the greatest zeal and diligence to attain perfection in the task he has laid out for himself. He must praise, love, and admire the work and virtues of others; and once he has made his choice, he must never leave the place of his profession. God is reached by many paths. Therefore, let each complete his own course with irrevocable concentration once he has chosen it so that he may become perfect by following this one

Conference 14.5-6; way.'*
PL 49:959-960.

If the cloistered profession becomes wearisome to you, remember Christ's patience and meekness when he was bound to the pillar for your sake. Over and over again ponder the saying of Jerome, 'If the solitude of the desert is upsetting you, take an imaginary stroll through paradise. For, as long as you are strolling in paradise, you will not be in the

Letter 14, to cloister.'*
Heliodorus;
PL 22:354.

When you hear the clappers being struck for work, think of Adam's first sin of disobedience and the punishment inflicted for it: 'Cursed is the ground because of you; in toil shall you eat its yield'.* Ponder in your mind his banishment from paradise, which filled him with sadness and grief. One may properly think that he almost died of weeping and wailing when he realized that he, who had lived in loveliness, in sunshine, in a place of sweet delights, had suddenly been cast out into so dark and terrible a prison, a land of drought and symbol of death. Remember also how hard Christ worked to bring you, the lost sheep, back to the heavenly flock and to reinstate you in paradise. 'Truly, he has borne our sins, our sorrow, and he was wounded for our iniquities'.* He grew tired of the load.* Pay attention and realize that there was no suffering like the suffering of him* who, for you, delivered his soul to death and for you was counted among the wicked.*

Gen 3:17.

Is 53:4,5.
Is 1:14.

Lam 1:12.

Is 53:12.

When you hear the signal summoning you to the monks' choir, bless and thank God that he has inivted you to the angels' table, to the music and harps of paradise, to the chanting of heaven. Thank him also that he opened to you the long-closed entrance of paradise, that by shedding his precious blood he put out the the fiery sword placed before its gates.*

Gen 3:24.

To him be honor and glory
forever and ever.
Amen.

HERE ENDS THE MIRROR
FOR THE NOVICES.

NOTES TO A MIRROR FOR NOVICES

1. The Cistercians bowed low toward each other while standing forward of their choirstalls whenever they said the first part of the doxology, 'Glory be to the Father and to the Son and to the Holy Spirit'; *Rituale Cisterciense* (Westmalle, 1949) 10. For the Cluniacs, see *Consuetudines Cluniacenses;* PL 149:702.

2. This probably refers to the 'familiar' psalms said for the extended monastic 'familiars'.

3. According to the *Meditations,* the complete formula was: 'Hail, holy, glorious, perpetual and loving Mother of God, Mary ever-Virgin, full of grace. The Lord is with you; blessed are you among women and blessed is the Lord Jesus, the sweet fruit of your blessed womb. Amen.' Cf. André Wilmart, *Auteurs spirituels* (Paris, 1932) 341.

4. A parallel text from the *Threefold Exercise* (On finishing the meditation) is, perhaps, a development of Alcuin's prayer. Cf. PL 101: 56. The Collect is taken from the Mass of the Holy Trinity. Cf. André Wilmart, 'Triple Exercise', RAM 11 (1930) 364, nn. 27-29.

5. According to the Statutes of the General Chapter, the Little Office of the Blessed Virgin was already recited in common as early as 1185, 'in the community and in the infirmary in this way. During the interval between Matins and Lauds Our Lady's Matins are held prior to the Office of the Dead, if it is then to be recited'. The remaining Hours of the *Marianum* followed the canonical Hours. 'They are omitted from the First Sunday of Advent to the Octave of Epiphany, from Palm Sunday to the Octave of Easter, from the Saturday before Pentecost Sunday to the next Saturday, within the Octave of the Assumption of the Blessed Virgin Mary [August 15] and on all feasts of twelve lessons'. Canivez, *Statuta,* 1185:28; 1191:75, 1194:1; 1195:102.

6. Stephen loved meditating on angels; see his long meditation in the *Threefold Exercise,* III, pp. 72-5.

7. *Our Daily Work (On Daily Work),* an anonymous english work edited by C. Horstmann, *Yorkshire Writers, Richard Rolle of Hampole,* 2 vols. (London, 1895-1896) 1:146-7, identifies this monk as Bernard: 'Sayn Bernard for the likying that he had in slike steryngs, gerned, that matyns tyme might have lasted til domesdai'. Cf. Geraldine Hodgson, *Rolle and 'Our Daily Work'* (London, 1929), Hope E. Allen, *Writings*

Ascribed to Richard Rolle, Hermit of Hampole and Materials for his Biography (London, 1927). According to *Our Daily Work,* St Bernard is given as the source for this anecdote. However, no such reference can be found in St Bernard's works. Cf. pp. 41-42, nn. 77, 78, 79 of the Introduction to Edmond Mikker's edition of the *Speculum Novitii, Collectanea OCR* 1-2 (1946), and P. Renaudin, *Quatre Mystiques Anglais* (Paris, 1945) 13-50.

8.   An allusion to St Jerome's *Letter to Eustochium;* PL 22:419-421: 'So ought to have appointed hours for prayer. . . . No one is ignorant that they are the third, sixth and ninth hour; at dawn also, and in the evening.' See *The Letters of St Jerome,* trans. C. C. Mierow, ed. T. C. Lawler (ACW 31; Westminster, 1963), 1:173.

9.   *Bucella*—originally the special but small loaf of white bread issued to the roman imperial bodyguard. They were the *buccellarii.* Cf. Aelred Jesu: *Quis dabit mihi buccellarum illarum mendicatarum participem fieri* (SCh. p. 6). This use of *bucella* is probably an allusion to the white loaf of bread and the whiteness of the Host. Cf. Baldwin, Sacr; SCh 94:471-569 on manna.

10.   For the cistercian chapter see Guignard, *Les monuments primitifs,* pp. 167-172. For the Cluniac chapter, see *Consuetudines Cluniacenses,* PL 149:734-737.

11.   Fish were served in refectory only as a *pitancia* ('treat'), although this suggests that they may have been fairly common by Stephen's day.

12.   Bread was made from wheat (*frumentum, triticum*), corn (*far*) which was ground and made into grits, rye (*sigalum*), barley (*hordeum*). The common bread (*panis communis*) used by peasants was a mixture of rye and barley. This was eaten in Cîteaux. Wheaten bread (*panis triticeus*) or pure wheaten bread was also called *panis albus* and was regarded as luxury at Cîteaux. The bread in general usage was a mixture of rye and wheat. See Roger Grand and Raymond Latouche, *Histoire d'agriculture au moyen age* (Paris, 1950) 315-322. The General Chapter of 1134 decreed that white bread was not to be baked in any cistercian house—not even for principal feasts. Instead, coarse bread (*panis communis*) was to be used. Canivez, *Statuta,* I, p. 16 (XIV). Cf. Aelred, Inst incl 12 (SCh 76:75-7; CF 2:59-60) for the food allowed to the recluse.

13.   See Edmond Mikkers' reference in *Collectanea OCR* 1-2 (1946) 35, n. 53, which provides an excellent and well-documented bibliographical note on this subject.

14.   *The Dialogues of St Gregory,* Book II (PL 66:125-204; 77:149-430) is the Life of St Benedict. For an excellent English translation, see *St Gregory the Great, Dialogues,* trans. O. J. Zimmerman, FCh 39 (New York, 1959).

15.   Aelred calls the Holy Scriptures 'The water sources of the springs of Wisdom', Inst incl 20 (SCh 76:93; CF 2:68). Cf. Adam of Perseigne, Ep 5 (*Lettres I*, trans. Jean Bouvet, SCh 66: 119, CF 21:102-104) 119, stresses the importance of Scripture in the formation of novices; William of Saint Thierry said that it 'nourishes with the fruit of spiritual knowledge' Cant 46; SCh 82:134; CF 6:36). See also Armand Veilleux, *La Liturgie dans le cénobitisme pachomien au quatrième siècle*, Studia Anselmiana, 57 (Rome, 1968) 266-75, for the study of Scripture in pachomian monasteries.

16.   Aelred, Inst incl 20; SCh 76:95; CF 2:68. The words of Stephen are taken practically verbatim from William of Saint Thierry's *Epistola ad Fratres de Monte Dei* (PL 184:327D; CF 12:52).

17.   *Letter 22 to Eustochium, 52 to Nepotianus, 58 to Paulinus, 122 to Rusticus*, PL 22:394-425, 527-540, 579-586; 1038-1046. *De laudibus vitae solitariae: Letter 14 to Heliodorus;* PL 22:347-355. See Mierow and Lawler for an English translation of the *Letters of St Jerome*, vol. I, in ACW 33:59-69.

18.   Stephen was well read in the works of Aelred.

19.   E. Mikkers, *Collectanea OCR* 8 (1946) 31, 40 discusses this story and its insertion into the cistercian menology. See Henriquez, *Menologium cisterciense* (Antwerp, 1630) 72, Herbertus, *De miraculis* 3.9 (PL 185:1358-80) and *Exordium magnum* 2.26 (PL 185:1032-34).

20.   The practice of relating the Hours of the Divine Office to Christ's life had become general by Stephen's time. See E. Mikkers, 'Introduction, *Collectanea* 8 (1946) 34, n. 52.

21.   This text is not to be found literally in St Jerome but the idea is analogous to that in *Commentarium in Isaiam* 5.21; PL 24:200: 'How quickly flees the hired laborer's year and he regards all labor as brief provided he attains the desired reward', or, *Commentarium in Ezechielem* 9.30; PL 25:290: 'When compared with eternity, all time is brief'. Compare also his *Letter to Philomena;* PL 26:650.

ON THE
RECITATION
OF THE
DIVINE OFFICE

ON THE RECITATION OF
THE DIVINE OFFICE

PROLOGUE

MY DEAR FRIEND, you asked me to draw up for you a plan for putting a check on the mind's wanderings. Your request caused me to feign ignorance and to keep silent for a long time. Actually I was only pretending to be silent, for I was aware of the dangers inherent in a subject where everybody is rich only in his own understanding and relies on his own experiences. Besides, it would be quite dangerous to impose on another a method of one's own ingrained preferences. We are aware that different methods of psalmody affect people in different ways.

For example, there are those who are well-trained in the spiritual life. They extract from the psalms meanings which may be mystical, moral, or anagogical. From them they fashion pleasant meditations which produce an aversion for the things of the world and a longing for the things of heaven. To them time spent reciting the psalmody—no matter how long and drawn out—always seem to pass quickly, and the burden seems light. To them the time seems scarcely long enough to squeeze the honey from the comb, that is, delightful meaning from the literal.

Lk 18:13.

Lk 18:38.

Antiphon of first vespers of the feast of the Circumcision, 1 January.

Ps 17:12.

Then there are others who briefly touch upon the literal meaning of the word, as long, that is, as the word, is on their lips. But, during the pauses they use greetings to the Blessed Mary or ejaculations like, 'God, be merciful to me, a sinner',* in order to stop the mind's wanderings. For instance, 'Christ Jesus, Son of the living God, have mercy on me'* during one pause, and 'Jesus, who deigned to be born of the Virgin, have mercy on me'* during another. Then they pick up the verse being recited on their side [of choir] and say the verse being recited by the opposite choir in silence.

Simpler souls constitute yet another category. They have not been given the gift of understanding the psalms, but find themselves, in so far as the understanding of the psalms and prophecies go, in 'dark, misty rain-clouds'.* Those so constituted usually conjure up imaginary pictures—like the Archangel Gabriel greeting the Virgin, the Virgin conceiving the Word, Mary greeting Elizabeth, John leaping for joy in Elizabeth's womb, Jesus being born of the Virgin, Jesus crying in the manger and gleaming toward heaven. As if by way of thanksgiving, they refer a verse of the Office to each of the great works which Christ performed up to the time of his passion. During Lauds they draw imaginary pictures of Christ crucified on the floorboards, or they say the five psalms in honor of his five wounds. Some of the simpler address the first three verses to the Holy Trinity, the next five wounds of Christ on the cross, and the other five to the five joys of the Blessed Virgin.

They may also refer nine verses to the nine orders of angels, twelve to the twelve apostles and other verses to the martyrs, confessors, virgins and all the saints familiar to them. Thus, in accordance with their capabilities, they make very good use of the time. We all know that some of them have advanced from such simplicity to high degrees of virtues.

So you see, my friend, it is very difficult for me to lay down a formula in these matters. Therefore, without doing violence to anybody's experience, I shall propose to you a few points based on my own inadequate and insufficient powers of comprehension about the first method, without prejudicing in any way more refined expectations.

My friend, during the recitation of the Office your main intention must be, as blessed Benedict said in his Rule, that your mind be in harmony with your voice.* This exercise is rather difficult at first, but in time it pays back handsomely in love and tranquility those who persevere in it. To help us in this effort our same Teacher has offered us the remedy of the psalmist's verse in the Night Office: 'At the middle of the night I will rise [to give you thanks]'.* For those who persevere abundant indeed will be his saving deeds; his graces '[are] like the mighty deep'.*

In view of the capacity of the simple with whose instruction we are now concerned, we ought to consider the four main aspects of God's saving deeds: creation; the new creation or redemption; the justification of sinners; and, the glorification of the just. To

RB 19.

Ps 118:62.

Ps 35:7, cf. Ps 77:15.

explain further: creation from nothing; redemption from hell; justification from mortal sin and shameful relapses; and, glorification from the mire of corruption. These are the foremost incentives for loving the Lord God. They make it easy for us to love him totally. They bind our devotion more gently, raise it more metely, draw it together more tightly, and fasten it more firmly.

'In his first work [the Creation]', says blessed Bernard, 'God gave me to myself. In the second [the Redemption] he gave me himself and by doing so he gave me back to myself. Thus given and returned, I am in debt to him for myself. But, what shall I return to the Lord* for himself? Even if I return myself a thousandfold, of what value am I to God?'* In creation, God gave us to ourselves when he endowed man with free will. He also gave himself to us because 'he created us in his own image and likeness'* and 'He let the light of his countenance shine upon us'.*

In his recreation he gave us first of all his Son in the incarnation, when 'unto us a child was born and a Son was given to us'.* Then he gave his only begotten Son to us in the passion. The Son likewise gave himself for us, and when he gave himself for us in the redemption, he gave us back to ourselves.

In the justification of sinners he gave us his Holy Spirit, both by forgiving our sins and by sharing the sacred mysteries. In an ineffable and loving movement of his will, the Holy Spirit deigned to unite our spirit soul with his infinite majesty; as has been written, 'Whoever is joined to the Lord becomes one spirit with

Ps 115:12.

Dil 15; SBOp 3: 132; CF 13:108.

Cf. Gen 1:26-27.

Ps 4:7.

Introit of the Third Mass of Christmas Day. Cf. Is 9:5.

him'.* Through his miraculous activity in our   *1 Cor 6:17.*
spirit, he renews our whole life.

In the glorification he gives us the Holy
Trinity in its entirety when, renewed in spirit
and glorified in body and soul, we shall
triumph in a state of everlasting happiness
and rejoice in both vestures because 'we shall
see him as he is' and God will be 'all in all'.*   *1 Jn 3:2;*
                                                    1 Cor 15:28.
My friend, these are the points you should
consider during the psalmody, because these
are the themes of the psalms. By 'creation' we
understand all the miraculous events of the
Old Testament up to the time of the incarnation of the Word. About them the psalms,
written at the time these events took place,
have much to say, especially in their literal
meaning. By 're-creation' [we understand]
Christ's incarnation, his life and teaching, his
passion, resurrection, ascension, the sending
of the Holy Spirit, his [second] coming and
the Last Judgment. By 'justification' [we
mean] the conversion of sinners, confession
and purification, the attainment of God's
mercy, the strength to counter all temptations, and zeal for all virtues. By 'glorification' [we mean] fellowship with the angels
and all the saints, the vision of God, knowledge of the truth, love and indescribable joy,
the blessed life and the continuous and everlasting praise of God as expressed by the
words 'Happy are they who dwell in your
house: they will praise you for ever and
ever'.*   *Ps 83:5.*

1. THE MEDITATION BEGINS

Ps 118:62.

My dear brother, when you arise in the middle of the night to praise the Lord,* recite first Matins of the Blessed Virgin with such devotion as if you were present at the birth of Jesus Christ. The general belief is that Christ was born at that hour of the night. Act as if you were addressing the Blessed Virgin. Direct your thoughts either to her or to her Son by means of the hymns, psalms, readings and responsories of the Office.

2. THE LORD'S PRAYER

Cf. Ph 4:6.

Once the bell has rung, the Lord's Prayer is said first, because first our petitions ought to be made known to God.* From him, and no one else, must we seek what we need.

3. THE CREED

Heb 11:6.

Next follows the creed because just as it is impossible to please God without faith,* so whatever is offered in faith cannot displease God. It is proper then that the Divine Office begin with a profession of faith, the foundation stone of all virtues.

4. MATINS

Ps 69:1.

During the opening words, 'O God, come to my assistance,'* ponder your own weakness and lack of strength. Say, 'Lord, I am no help to myself, I can do nothing by myself. But you, Lord, are all powerful: "Come, therefore, to my assistance; Lord, make haste to help me;" or else I shall fail, lacking the strength to persevere'.*

Cf. Est 15:6.
Ps 50:17

While 'O Lord, open my lips'* is being said

for the first time, think of God the Father, the Creator of all things. And at 'and my mouth shall proclaim your praise', praise him for creation. At the second 'O Lord [ponder] God the Son, redeemer of the world; at 'open my lips' praise him for recreation. At the third 'O Lord' [think of] the Holy Spirit; at 'open my lips', praise him for the justification of sinners. It is important to admit your own wretchedness, because without God you could not even open your lips.

5. AN EXPOSITION OF PSALM THREE

'O Lord, how are they increased who trouble me.'* See why the psalmist called out with great urgency, 'Lord, make haste to help me'. For 'many rise up against me. Many are saying of me "there is no salvation for him in God".'* Many are your past crimes, many your present temptations and tribulations, and many the demons lying in wait. 'But you, O Lord, are my shield in the Son's incarnation; you are 'my glory' in his resurrection, and 'you lift up my head'* in his ascension. Thus I have no reason to lack confidence when 'I call out to the Lord with my voice',* in confessing my sins or singing his praises. 'And he answers me', he pours out the hope of forgiveness just as soon as I have confessed my sins.

'I have slept and taken my rest', I have tarried long in sins great and small. But 'I have risen up because the Lord has protected me',* through his mercy alone and not through any merit on my part. 'I shall not fear the myriads of people arrayed against me on

Ps 3:2.

Ps 3:2-3.

Ps 3:4.

Ps 3:5.

Ps 3:6.

Ps 3:7-8.

every side' rise up, O Lord, that is, if you rise up, O Lord [and save me, O my God]'.* 'I shall not be afraid because you strike all my enemies'; because You use the rod of your cross, because through your holy passion you fought and defeated all my adversaries and all the evil spirits.

Ps 3:8.

'You have broken the teeth of the wicked',* that is, you have destroyed all the pleasures, all the silly thoughts, and all the riches of this world which continue to tempt me, to gnaw

Ps 3:9.

at me. 'Salvation is the Lord's',* not in this world or in the flesh or in being thought learned or holy; rather, 'let him who would

1 Cor 1:31;
2 Cor 10:17.

boast, boast in the Lord'.*

This is why every psalm ends with 'Glory be to the Father, and the Son and the Holy Spirit'. Every good work and every prayer must be referred back to the Holy Trinity as their efficient cause. There is no other hope or salvation because 'the help of man is worth-

Ps 59:13.

less'.*

Therefore do I bow down before you, O Holy Trinity, because you spread out your grace and blessing over your people bowed down in supplication.

6. THE INVITATORY

Here are two meditations on the Invitatory.

[I.] If we look at the work of Creation and invite the citizens of heaven to help us praise the Creator, it is as if we were saying,

Sir 15:9.

'Unseemly is praise on a sinner's lips';* come, therefore, citizens of heaven and members of God's household, who stand uninterruptedly in the blessed vision of God, who endlessly praise him and 'give him no silence',* 'come, let us sing joyfully to the Lord,' who created us out of nothing. 'Come, let us sing joyfully to the Lord'* who bought us back from hell; 'let us greet him with thanksgiving'* for our redemption from sin, and 'let us joyfully sing psalms to him', foretasting just a little, in the sweetness of devotion, the first fruits of our coming joy.

'The Lord is a great God.'* Admire his power, for he did not forsake his people. Admire the immensity of his kindness and mercy; he who has no need of anyone has expended such great mercy on the angels and men. 'His is the sea . . . '* Admire the depths of his wisdom. 'Oh that today you would hear his voice'* and 'forty years I loathed that generation'*: think of his amazing patience and of his strict justice at the Last Judgment.

During the Invitatory he appears to us as a familiar acquaintance. We consider how he created us anew. Prompted by fraternal love, we invite the brethren to reflect on the work of our redemption.

[II.] On feast days when the Invitatory is being chanted aloud by two brothers standing before the altarstep *gradus**—picture the choir of patriarchs and prophets proclaiming the coming of Christ and singing 'Come, "all you who are weary and heavy laden,"* let us sing joyfully to the Lord; let us rejoice in God our Saviour,'* lying in a crib. 'Let us greet him while he is a child with thanksgiving, let us joyfully sing psalms to him' who is kind and meek, before he comes, mighty and awesome. And if someone were to ask, 'Will

Cf. Is 62:7.

Ps 94:1.

Ps 94:2.

Ps 94:3.

Ps 94:6.

Ps 94:8.
Ps 94:10.

*Rituale Cisterciense (Westmalle, 1949) 87. Cf. Guignard, 162.

Mt 11:28.

Ps 94:1.

the day come when he who is now small and
humble will be awesome?', I will answer him,
'Yes, it will, because the Lord is a great God
Ps 94:3.   and a great king above all gods'.* He is not
only mighty but also merciful, 'because the
Ps 94:14.   Lord does not reject His people.'* He is
mighty, 'for in his hands [are the depths of
Ps 94:7   the earth],'* and he is wise, as I have ex-
plained above. 'His is the sea [for he has made
Ps 94:5.   it],'* that is, he is long-suffering; he overlooks
Wis 11:23.   the sins of men that they may repent.*
Accordingly, 'if you hear his voice today,
Ps 94:8.   harden not your hearts'.* 'I swore in my
Ps 94:11.   anger':* he will render just retribution at the
Last Judgment. The words on judgment are
followed by the doxology [Glory be . . .] in-
dicating that we must thank and praise God
not only in good times but also in bad. For all
his deeds are just and all his ways are mercy
Tob 3:2.   and truth.*

7. THE FERIAL HYMN
'Eternal Maker of All Things.' During this
hymn we should reflect on God who in his
mercy lowered himself to the level of our
fickle nature and, though eternal and outside
time, set up our seasons in order to relieve our
boredom. In the hymn the soul praises God,
using the temporal world as its vehicle. As the
darkness of night comes before dawn, before
the watchman announces the coming of the
new day at night's end, as the morning star
makes its appearance and then daylight, so
there was night before the revelation of grace.
But, as the Apostle said, 'The night has
Rom 13:12.   passed [and day is at hand]'.* During this

night the herald of the day—that is, the herald
of the time of grace—has spoken. The choir of
the prophets was such a night lamp for
travelers,* because the time of the prophets
was like a rain-cloud.† This [morning star]
'separated night from night', that is to say,
he purged the evil from your midst.* This
victorious morning star, our Lord Jesus Christ,
made flesh and born, brought true light to
the world; as he himself said, 'I am the light
of the world'.* It brought an end to darkness:
gone are the dark and misty rain-clouds of the
past; now many vagrants return to the right
path. To his eyes all things are naked and out
in the open; nothing escapes their intensity.*
'It is a sure guide for all sailors,' that is, for
the   pastors   who   administer   a   particular
church. 'It calms the foaming billows,' that is,
the secular powers, so that they cannot injure
the Church no matter how much they might
want to. 'Even the very Church's Rock melts
at the crowing of the cock.' Firmly believing
in Christ's incarnation and in the actions
which he performed while in the flesh, the
Church—on the authority of this rock—ab-
solves all sins, according to his words, 'What-
soever you declare bound on earth shall be
bound in heaven . . . ' .* 'O let us vigorously
arise'. Action is needed, and this comes not
from   indolence   but   from   vigor.   For
the lazy, the coddled, the undisciplined will
not reach the kingdom of God. Rather, the
violent will seize it.* 'The cock'—that is, the
ranks of the apostles and confessors—'rebukes
our slumbering eyes', bestirs the lazy 'who
still in sleep would lie / And shames who

*Cf. Jb 20:8;
33:15.
†Ps 17:12.

Deut 17:8f.

Jn 8:12.

Ps 18:7. Cf. Heb
4:13.

Mt 16:19.

Mt 11:12.

would their Lord deny'. The preaching of the truth gives 'new hope' to sinners and 'Sickness the feeble frame forsakes'. They are given the strength to resist habitual sins. 'The robber sheathes his lawless sword': the devil's power to tempt is greatly weakened. 'Faith is once again restored' to those who had fallen into despair and unbelief.

Whence this great power of preaching, if not from Jesus?* 'Look, Jesus, on your trembling servants', for no teaching is effective without you. 'If you but look, our sins are gone,' just as you looked at Peter and he wept bitterly. 'If you but look' with those holy eyes with which you looked on your mother from the cross, 'our sins are gone and with due tears our pardon won'. 'Cast through our hearts your piercing ray': this explains all the preceding. 'Your name be first on every tongue', that is, first in time and in importance, in confessing our praise; then we shall 'loosen our lips to you' in confessing our sins. But even when we do all things well, we should always say, 'We are useless servants'.* Let us praise him for all this: 'Glory be to God the Father, to the Son, and to the Holy Spirit. Amen.'

On saints' feast days, because the hymn is a praise of God, when we sing the hymn we should praise God in his saints and the saints in God, by recalling his glorious miracles in the life of the apostles and apostolic men, the great endurance of the martyrs, the saintly lives and forbearance of confessors, and the purity of virgins. Inspired by them, let us endeavor, in so far as we can, either to

*Cf. Bernard, SC 15.6; SBOp 1:85; CF 4:109.

Lk 17:10.

imitate or to admire them. Let us imitate their virtues and admire their miracles. This we must also do during the psalms, antiphons, readings and responsories on saints' feast days. This is how the text of psalms should be used, as God has ordained.

If anyone is so simple that he is unable to connect the psalm with these themes, let him at least meditate between psalms on the four items mentioned before and thus seek the fellowship of the saints. I believe his efforts shall not remain fruitless.

8. THE FERIAL PSALMS

Blessed Benedict quite properly began the Night Office on Sunday with the twentieth psalm.* That psalm deals with Christ's two natures and with his royal power: 'O Lord, in your strength', that is, in your divinity, 'the King', that is, Christ in his human nature, 'will rejoice'. 'He will greatly rejoice in his victory'. He is the saving help and Saviour of the whole world. 'You have granted him his heart's desire'. He does whatever he pleases and he saves all whom he wishes to save. Blessed therefore, is the recipient of his favor, 'for you welcomed him with choice blessings', you anointed him with the fullness of blessing and grace long before the Fall. 'You placed on his head a crown of pure gold', that is to say, the everlasting glory of perfect union and indivisible God-head. He asked eternal 'life of you' and you gave him and all his followers 'length of days', that is, everlasting happiness. 'Great is his glory in your victory . . .' that is to say, the achievement of our salvation

RB 18.

through his incarnation, his poverty, his care
in preaching, his miracle-working, his institu-
tion of the sacraments, his obedience even unto death, and above all, in his Passion and the
redemption of the whole world. 'You conferred upon him majesty and splendor' in his
glorious resurrection. 'You will make him
blessed forever' at his ascension. 'You will
gladden him with the joy of your presence' at
the Last Judgment when he will be seated on
your right hand. He will sit in his completely
glorified body at the Last Judgment, at the
Last Accounting, when we shall look for that
Eph 4:13.   perfect man [Who is Christ].* And he will
hand over his kingdom to God the Father,
1 Cor 15:28.   and God will be all in all.* The prophet
revealed the background of all this when he
said, 'the king hopes in the Lord . . . ' , which
means that he did not place his hope in himself. He said the same also in another psalm.
'Because he hopes in me I,' the Lord, 'will
deliver him; I will protect him because he has
known my name. With length of days I will
content him, and 'I will show him my salvation'. 'May your hand find all who hate
you . . . ' Here he is speaking about the majesty of the king and he adds something about
the punishment of his enemies. 'May your
right hand find all who hate you', that is,
may your left hand be armed with this world's
whip and your right hand with eternal vengeance. It is as if he were saying: those who
now scorn him desirable and humble, will one
day feel him terrible and vengeful.

The psalmist describes how this whip will
be used when he says, 'You will make them

burn as though in a fiery furnace on the day
of your wrath,' that is to say, on the day of
your judgment. While he now overlooks our
sins so that we may repent,* then he will take   *Wis 11:23.*
on a look of wrath, when he metes out
punishments. And, to be enclosed in a blazing
furnace is to be so completely engulfed by
fire that one can never get away from it no
matter which way one turns. There is there
no corner left in which to hide. The words
'blazing furnace' well describe the pain of
everlasting damnation from freezing waters
to oppressive heat, and the fact that there is
never a surcease of unending torment. Hence
the following words, 'The Lord will engulf
them in his anger'. This agony knows no
respite. 'Fire will devour them', that is, it will
swallow them completely; it will not consume
them but it will wholly pervade them. He will
'wipe out their fruit from the land' of the
living by depriving them of all hope, 'and their
posterity from among the sons of men', so
that they will not be reckoned [among the
number of the elect]. For 'they have plotted
evil'—the evil of your passion—'against you;
they have devised wicked schemes which
cannot succeed' to remove any remembrance
of Christ from the earth. The sentence of all
these evildoers is, 'You shall put them to
flight; you shall aim your shaft against them',
which means: you will not look on them with
favor and grace, but leave them to their own
devices, 'O Lord, rise up in your power.' It is
as if he were saying, 'This is how it will be
with the wicked' while you, O Lord, sur-
rounded by your entire household will arise

after the Last Judgment in the full power of
your divine glory. Then we will forever sing
and 'chant and sing psalms of your might'.

Glory be to God the unbegotten Father
who did not spare his own Son but handed
him over for us sinners. Glory be to his only
begotten Son who for our sake became
obedient to the Father, even unto death.
Glory be to the Holy Spirit who descended
on men in the form of tongues of fire to
enlighten the whole human race and to direct
it towards the true light. This is what you
should think about as you say the *Gloria* at
the end of each psalm.

Here it is, my dear brother: I have stated
briefly and without prejudice my various
thoughts on this psalm in order to demonstrate
concisely how you can reap profit from the
other psalms. I cannot mull over each and every
other psalm in this manner, but a word to the
wise will suffice and satisfy the sincere seeker.
He who said, 'Ask and you shall receive, seek
and you will find, knock and it shall be opened
Mt 7:7; Lk 11:9. to you',* and will increase your understanding.

You should also know, dear brother, that
metaplasm, or the interchange of persons and
things, is of frequent occurrence in the psalms.
At times one verse speaks of the members
and another verse of the head, one about those
who continue in sin and another about those
doing penance, one about the glorification of
the just and another about the wailing of
misery. You will often see such examples
in the same verse, not only in the same
psalm. Therefore, when there is a change of
persons, change your interpretation, too.

You must transfer the things which you cannot understand readily about the members to
the head; then you will understand them. For
instance, the verse 'Judge me, O Lord, according to my justice and according to the inno-
cence that is in me';* or, 'I have run [the   *Ps 7:9.*
course] and I have loved without iniquity',*   *Ps 58:5.*
and other such verses. Apply to the members
and not to the Head the passage 'I acknowl-
edge my wickedness and my sin is before me
always,'* and many other such passages.   *Cf. Ps 50:5*

I do not want you greatly to belabor*   *Cf. Rom 16:6.*
these points just for the sake of exercising
the mind or of drawing fine intellectual dis-
tinctions. Instead, I want you to search in
them and extract from them the sweetness of
affection which they experience on whom
God bestowed the gift of meditating on the
psalms.

Meditation is a reflection on the facts and
individual circumstances of God's saving
deeds, for the purpose of arousing the mind
to experience the deep affections of joy and
love or—on the other hand—of fear, wonderment, longing, praise and similar sentiments.

Here is an example:

9. MEDITATION ON PSALM 20
We have already said a few words about the
meaning of this psalm. If you wish to meditate on it, ponder, when you hear the verse,
'O Lord, in your strength the King rejoices',
who that king really is. He is Christ, the King
of Kings and Lord of Lords, the ruler of all
because through him all things came into

Jn 1:3.
1 Pet 1:12.

Col 2:3.

Ps 44:3.
Jn 7:46.

Cf. Ps 44:3.

Cf. 1 Mac 4:58.
Ps 138:6.

Is 24:16.

being and apart from him nothing came to be.* Think of his beauty, a beauty which the angels yearn to behold.* Think of the singular holiness, in his union with the Word. Think of his wisdom about sin, because in him there are hidden all reserves of wisdom and knowledge.* Think of his eloquence, because grace is poured out on his lips* and never has anyone spoken like this man.* These or other such reflections will produce a tender affection of love or yearning in the soul. This is not surprising, for, if he is the fairest among the sons of men,* the most finely featured, the wisest, the most chaste and the most dutiful, should he not be loved and sought out above and beyond everybody and everything else?

If you go on with your meditation, you should examine next the nature and the depth of the joy in which this king rejoices in the power he received from God the Father. What does the soul say? Such joy and knowledge is too wonderful for me;* I cannot attain to it.* Indeed, who can understand those wondrous outpourings, those ineffable raptures, those tenderest feelings which that blessed soul of Christ, the unique wisdom of God, experienced? This is truly his secret.* But if we cannot experience it, we can still admire it and take delight in the great glory of our Redeemer.

In like manner, consider how the Father 'welcomed him with goodly blessings' and how and in what manner he 'placed on his head a crown of pure gold'. How insensitive, how unhappy will be the soul which does not reach out to taste the sweet joy, the glory, and the beauty of the king who, clothed in light as a garment,* mercifully deigns to share his robe of glory and immortality. For, 'he asked life' from God, not only for Himself but also for His followers, and the Father 'granted it'* and 'did not withhold the request of his lips'.* Pondering in meditation and longing for this immortal life, the soul contemplates that 'length of days forever and ever'* where there is no fear of death but a state of unending happiness, and no fear or worry, but the full recognition of truth in love.

Ps 103:2.

Ps 20:5.

Ps 20:3.

Ps 20:5.

Then, changing the subject, the psalm ends the meditation hastily on a note of fear, dealing with the punishment of his enemies.* For hope without fear develops into presumption, and fear without hope leads into despair; hence hope and fear often go hand in hand in the psalms. This is why after promising to the king 'who put his trust in the Lord' that 'by favor of the most high his reign shall be unshaken,' the psalm adds, 'your hand will unmask all your enemies', and the remaining words of the psalm, which all instill fear, but especially the words 'make them burn as though in a fiery furnace', when you appear [in judgment]. The day on which he will judge—that is, the day of the Last Judgment—is a day of wrath. Its fear often inspires the following meditation:

Ps 20:9-12.

Visualize the vengeful judge whose glance nobody can withstand, as he comes in the clouds of heaven with trumpets while the earth and the heavens are all ablaze, the angels tremble and the dead arise, tottering

Cf. Jb 9:19.

in their naked bodies. Then the verdict will
be given from which there is no appeal and
nobody will dare to bear witness on another's
behalf.* Consider further, how the evidence
of an accusing conscience will be presented
when the books are opened wide, and every
evil deed we performed during our lifetime
will be laid bare. See how the door of mercy
will be closed and the prison of hell wide
open and offering no escape. Think, also, of
all the torments: the intolerable stench, the
freezing cold, the great heat, and innumerable others like them. Think of the bar-
barous jailors eager to inflict punishments:
torments without a moment's let-up, without
end, without moderation. And, finally, how
bitter it is to be shut out forever from the joy
of divine contemplating, to be excluded from
the blessed companionship of the saints, to
be an outcast from the heavenly homeland,
to be excluded from a life of happiness in
heaven and be condemned to a life of
eternal death.

Dwell often on these thoughts and on
others like them. Cultivate in your soul the
fear of God in order to rid yourself of all
carnal temptations, for it is written, 'The fear
of the Lord drives out sin'.* The psalmist
expressed this succinctly when he said, 'Make
them burn as though in a fiery furnace', when
he referred to the punishment and the en-
gulfing fire, and 'May the Lord consume them
in his anger,'* referring to the Judge's anger
and to the total confusion of the defendants.
He also said, 'Fire will devour them', which is
a reference to the perpetuity of eternal

Sir 1:27.

Ps 20:10.

damnation and, 'You will destroy their fruit
from the earth,'* an allusion to disinheritance
from the kingdom of heaven.

Ps 20:10,11

My dear brother, this is the way to proceed
also in the other psalms. I cannot spend as
much time on each of the other psalms
because it would take too long and tire the
reader.

The theme is more easily understood and
the path to meditation is much more smooth
when the psalms treat the actions of the
Incarnate Christ, for his power and his glorified immortality are not accessible to us.
Thus you will find it easy to meditate on the
earthly life of Christ, his humility and poverty, his teaching and miracles, his mercy
toward sinners and his obedience in accepting
sufferings, the cross, and his death. Visualize
Christ as if he were doing or suffering these
things before your very eyes, for, as St Augustine said, whenever we recall Christ's passion,
he is, so to say, killed anew in each instance.*

*Cf. Augustine,
Cnofessions,
FCh 21:327ff.*

If you look closely, you will also find in the
psalms plenty of material for meditating on
your own wretchedness, your sinful past, your
ingratitude, and your carelessness.

The best form of meditation is to use the
psalms, hymns, and canticles in praise of the
Lord and of his mercy, and to oppose it to our
own negligence and wretchedness; also, to
make a comparison between his benefits and
our ingratitude. St Bernard bequeathed this
way to us when he said, 'I have material
aplenty for meditation: my own sins and
God's goodness to me'.*

*Cf. Dil 3 (SBOp
3:124; CF 13:95-6),
SC 11 (SBOp 1:
48ff.; CF 4:
69-76).*

Although I am not able to explain the

individual psalms as they follow in sequence, I do want to lay before you—briefly and without prejudging any other interpretation—a theme in each psalm which can be the starting point for meditation. I do this for the benefit of the simple who may find it difficult to have recourse to original commentaries for each meditation.*

10. THEMES OF THE PSALMS
[FOR SUNDAY MATINS]

The theme of the twentieth psalm, 'O Lord, in your strength [the king is glad]', is Christ the King, in his two natures. Everybody can see that it deals with both his natures, the divine and the human.

It is well followed by the twenty-first psalm, 'My God, who have you forsaken me?', which treats mainly Christ's passion. For, the incarnate Christ's main task was our redemption through his Passion.

There follows [the twenty-second psalm], 'The Lord is my shepherd', which lists the blessings God offers us through Christ; such are the graces, mentioned in different places of the psalm, which prepare us in this life for eternity. After the psalm which death dealt with the passion, this psalm properly follows, because it is through Christ's passion that the perfection of a good life is obtained.

Psalm twenty-three, 'The earth is the Lord's', has as its subject matter the glorification of Christ and man's restoration through his resurrection, crowned by the perfection of this present life.

[Psalm twenty-four], 'To you I lift up my

soul, O Lord,' aptly continues the same theme,
namely the glorification of Christ and the
redemption of mankind. It expresses the desire of the faithful soul to depart from
Babylon, this place of misery, and go up
to Jerusalem.

[Psalm twenty-five], 'Give sentence on me,
O Lord, [for I have walked in integrity]',
speaks of the person who left his evil com-
panions and clings to the good.

[Psalm twenty-six], 'The Lord is my
light', is the first psalm of the second Nocturn. It deals with a twofold anointing or
smearing-on of oil: the oil of baptism, which
causes the faithful soul to rejoice that it has
been anointed and its sins forgiven; and the
anointing for immortality used in the anointing of kings, realizing that what has already
taken place in the Head will also take place in
the members. This is grace given in return for
grace—the grace of glorification in return for
the grace of justification. Having considered
the benefits listed in the preceding five
psalms, the faithful soul will burst forth into
exultant praise and say, 'The Lord is my
light [and my salvation]'.

[Psalm twenty-seven], 'To You, O Lord,
shall I call', reviews Christ's passion and resurrection in very few words. Whatever love
and joy it inspires is attributed to God.

[Psalm twenty-eight] 'Give to the Lord',
follows and deals with the completion of the
Tabernacle, that is, of the Church, which
reaches completion in the seven gifts of the
Holy Spirit, which give the Church strength
and security in the midst of this present evil.

Because our actions in this life, no matter how great they are, must be done in a spirit of faith—since it is impossible to please God without faith—psalm [twenty nine], 'I will extol you, O Lord', follows. Its main concern is Christ's resurrection. To explore the resurrection spiritually, one must resort to contemplation.

[Psalm thirty], 'In you, O Lord, have I hoped', is added next. It is a moral psalm; its theme is the mind's raptures and ecstacies which are of frequent occurrence whenever God speaks to the soul or man cultivates an attitude of holy fear.

[Psalm thirty-one], 'Happy is he [whose fault is taken away, whose sin is covered]', aptly follows next. It is a penitential psalm; its theme the proper attitude of the penitent who attributes whatever good there is in himself to God's grace rather than to any strength of his own. No one has this attitude unless God has revealed it to him. This is why *Is 33:2ff.* Isaiah, having seen the glory of the Lord,* fully recognized and regretted his own wretchedness.

11. MONDAY MATINS

The first psalm [is psalm thirty-two], 'Exult you just in the Lord'. It is a moral psalm, dealing with God's mercy. Thus it states at the outset 'the earth is full of the mercy of the Lord' and at the end, 'May your mercy, O Lord, be upon us [who have put our trust *Verses 2 and 5.* in you'.* The just man received such mercy when he was given power over all creatures in *Gn 1:28.* paradise.*

For this, God must be praised above and beyond all else. Accordingly, psalm [thirty-three], 'I will bless the Lord at all times', is said next, insisting that we must ever praise him in all his creatures and for all his acts of mercy. This psalm shows a good way of praising him and of showing gratitude, because tribulation is undergone and their liberation undertaken: 'Many are the troubles of the just man [but out of them all the Lord delivers him]'. It also encourages the petitioner—who is reminded that he has been heard on numerous occasions—as the passage relates, 'I sought the Lord and he answered me [and delivered me from all my fears]' to the words 'Come, children, listen to me . . . ' .*   *Verses 20, 5, 12.*
The psalm employs transferences, such as David for Christ, circumcision for baptism, and the sacrifice of the Old Law for the sacrament of [Christ's] Body and Blood. It also treats the transference of the priesthood and the kingdom of the Jews from the Jews to the Gentiles, for whom all the faithful—that is, the Church—rise up in thanksgiving and praise, saying: 'I will bless [the Lord at all times; his praise shall be forever in my mouth'.

But as his own spittle ran down on David's beard,* so some indignant and incredulous   *1 Sam 21:13.*
persons found the Saviour's words silly and insipid when he said, 'If you do not eat [the Flesh of the Son of Man and drink His Blood you have no life in you]'.*   *Jn 6:54.*
This is a repetition of the story of Achish,* the prototype   *1 Sam 21:10-15.*
of those who lack faith.

[Psalm thirty-four], 'Plead my cause, O

Lord, against those who harm me' follows,
because all those who want to live in Christ
suffer persecution. This psalm, whose subject
matter is Christ's suffering, is a prayer against
persecutors. Its purpose is to give quick
encouragement to those who are persecuted,
to help them bear their persecutors with
greater patience. Whenever you cannot apply
passages of this psalm to your own trials and
tribulations, apply them instead to the sufferings of Christ. By considering them, you will
be inspired to feel loving compassion or to
perform acts of penance.

The next psalm [thirty-six], 'be not vexed
[over evildoers, not jealous of those who do
wrong]', is highly moral. Its theme is the
complaint of some about the prosperity of
the evil and the misfortune of the good, as if
God paid no attention to earthly matters. But
the just man, overcoming all such notions,
freely proclaims at the end [of the psalm]
'the Lord will save the just; he will give them
aid [in time of distress]'. He will do what is
stated in the following verses 'because they
have put their hope in him'.*

Ps 36:39f., 37:16.

[Psalm thirty-seven], 'O Lord, in your
anger [punish me not]', follows quite rightly
for, after all this has been taken into account,
there is nothing of greater value than to think
back on one's sins and to do penance for
them. The psalm's theme is the sinner who
atones and grieves both in body and soul. It is
therefore called a penitential psalm.

In the second Nocturne, the first psalm
[is psalm thirty-eight], 'I said: "I will watch
my ways [so as not to sin with my tongue]"'.'

It recalls Jeduthun,* who overcame the world and what is in it and reached out in hope for things eternal. It properly follows the preceding psalm [thirty-seven] because [it shows how] true penance gives rise in the soul to contempt of the world. *Cf. 2 Chr 5:12.*

[Psalm thirty-nine,] follows no less appropriately: 'I have waited, waited for the Lord [and he heard my cry]'. It considers the exchange of the Old Testament for the New, of the old life for the new good way of life in which one must follow the will of God and not go off recklessly on one's own way.

Psalm [forty], follows 'Happy is he who has regard [for the lowly and the poor]', which deals with the Son of Korah, that is, with those who imitate Christ's humility and suffering. By studying these closely, the soul will be led to contemn this world and look for the glory to come.

However, because the intervening period should not be a time of idleness but one of longing, psalm [forty-one], 'Just as [the hind longs for the running waters, so my soul longs for you, O Lord]', is placed next. It expresses a longing for the invisible world of God and for eternal happiness.

Because eternal happiness is won through patience and martyrdom, psalm [forty-three], 'O God, our ears have heard', follows. It deals with the martyrs who on realizing they were to suffer gave thanks and, to comfort themselves in their present tribulations, recalled the favors which had been given to the Fathers in ancient times.

For the sake of comforting them, psalm

[forty-four], 'My heart overflows [with a goodly word],' is added. Its theme is the bridegroom and bride, that is, Christ and the Church, and those who are to be transformed from the Law to grace, that is, from the oldness of Adam to the newness of Christ.

12. TUESDAY

The first psalm [of the first Nocturn begins]

Ps 42:1. 'God is our refuge and our strength'.* Its themes are the hidden designs of God, that is, the mystery of the incarnation of the Word, the blindness of the Jews, and the illumination of the Gentiles.

The next psalm, very properly [is psalm forty-six], 'All you peoples [clap your hands, shout to God with cries of gladness].' It deals with the salvation and the consequent exaltation of the Gentiles.

And because the Church is founded on the Gentiles, psalm [forty-seven], 'Great is the Lord [and wholly to be praised in the city of God]', follows. Its theme is the firmament,*

Gen 1:1. that is, the Church, which it calls 'city' because of the solidarity and security of those who dwell in it. The psalm treats in a broader sense the incarnation and birth of Christ, the virginal birth and the adoration of the Magi, that is to say, the time when the Church was founded and joined with Christ its head, just as God created the firmament on the second day.

And since the boyhood and life of Christ invite us above all to a life of humility and poverty, psalm [forty-eight], 'Hear this, all you peoples [harken all who dwell in the world]', follows next. It urges contempt for the things of the world lest any of the faithful build his hope on things transitory.

Appropriately, [Psalm forty-nine] follows: 'The God of gods [has summoned the earth from the rising of the sun to its setting]'. It considers the end and termination of the sacrifice of the Law. In the Law, worldly possessions were given in sacrifice; in the grace of the New Testament, their place is taken by Christ. Anticipating this, the psalmist foresaw that the shadow as well as the substance of the [Old Law's] rituals will cease with the coming of grace.

The next psalm [fifty-one] goes on: 'Why do you glory in evil, [you champion of infamy]?' Its theme is anti-Christ and his adherents. After recalling the sacrifices of the Law, the psalmist turned his gaze to the anti-Christ who will make similar attempts to do away with all rival sacrifices. Our psalm excoriates this.

The first psalm in the second Nocturn [is psalm fifty-two], 'The fool said in his heart, there is no God.' Dealing with Amalek* and Ziklag,† its theme is conversion. It shows how from the mire of unbelief the Church has turned to God, and refutes the errors of blasphemers.

*Ex 17:8-16, 1 Sam 15:1-9.

†1 Sam 27:6.

The next psalm [fifty-three], 'O God, by your name [save me and by your might defend my cause]' shows how the faithful people dwelling in Ziph,* that is, among infidels, are hoping for liberation by the Lord.

1 Sam 23:14-24.

The following psalm [fifty-four], 'Harken,

O God, [to my prayer, turn not away from my pleading]', treats of the martyrs amidst persecution. It enumerates their manifold tribulations, and then lists their consolations lest the weak-spirited fall by the wayside in adversities.

Psalm [fifty-five], 'Have mercy on me, O God, for men trample upon me', has as its subject matter the Church detained in Geth,* that is weighed down by the pressures of this world, for Geth means wine press.*

1 Sam 21:10.

*Jerome, Liber interpretatione hebraicorum nominum 27.25; CCh 72:94.

A psalm [fifty-seven] dealing with the separation of the good from the evil aptly follows: 'Do you indeed pronounce justice and judge fairly, you men of rank?' Its theme is the rejection of the Jews and the establishment of the kingdom of Christ.

The next psalm [fifty-eight], 'Rescue me [from my enemies, O my God]', deals more fully with this establishment [of Christ's kingdom]. Its theme is Christ, as he speaks about the liberation he has effected, now in himself, now in his members, and of the calling of the Gentiles and the blinding of the Jews.

13. WEDNESDAY

The subject of the first psalm [fifty-nine], 'O God, You have rejected us', is the changeover from the old Adam to the new Christ and the trials inherent in this change.

Psalm [sixty], 'Hear my cry, O Lord', follows next and deals with the universal Church which, like an individual laboring in the midst of evil and hoping to be set free by Christ, cries out to the Lord from the farthest ends of the earth. This cry is called up by his longing for life eternal.

And so we move to psalm [sixty-one], 'Only in God [is my soul at rest]', which discusses the man who exchanges his secular outlook for a spiritual outlook, whom neither the love of things of this world nor the fear of death can keep from moving on quickly from things of the earth to the things of heaven.

The next psalm [sixty-five], 'Shout joyfully to God, all the earth', voices this desire and the inexpressible exaltation of mind the people are said to experience at Christ's resurrection.

The following psalm [sixty-seven], 'God arises [his enemies are scattered]', continues to deal with the joys of the resurrection. It talks about the exultation of Christ and of his Church consequent upon his resurrection and ascension; and about the knowledge and wisdom poured into the Apostles by the Holy Spirit, and about the ordering of the Church by diverse [ecclesiastical] ranks. However, the psalm does not do all this in its proper sequence.

And so psalm [sixty-eight], 'Save me, O God [for the waters threaten my life]', follows. Its theme is the second change-over, from mortality to immortality, through Christ's sufferings. The first change-over was from immortality to mortality, caused by Adam's sin.

The next psalm [sixty-nine], 'O Lord, come to my assistance', clearly fits in well here. It recalls how God's help saved the martyrs and confessors from hidden and open snares. The martyrs endured the lions, that is, the persecutors everybody saw; the confessors endured the dragons, that is, the persecutors nobody saw.

The faithful therefore rises to give thanks, as expressed with the words of the following psalm, 'In You, O Lord, have I hoped'. This psalm [seventy] praises God for the gifts of his grace.

And since all grace has its origin in Christ, psalm [seventy-one] comes next: 'O God, with your judgment [endow the king] . . . '. It talks about Christ according to his dual natures.

Marvelling at God's inconceivable goodness, the next psalm [seventy-two], 'How good God is to Israel' has as its theme the error of the simple-minded who, in their ignorance, do not understand the deep counsel of God who distributes the goods of this world indiscriminately to both the good and the bad.

14. THURSDAY

The first psalm [is Psalm seventy-three], 'O God, why have you cast us off forever'. Its theme is the destruction of the earthly Jerusalem with all its legal claims, as the prophet foresaw in spirit. It is a psalm of lamentation bewailing the final capture of the city by Titus and Vespasian.*

AD 70.

The psalm that follows [seventy-four], 'We give you thanks [O God]', deals with the humility the prophet sought to inculcate when he spoke of sorrows to be endured for the hope of happiness to come.

Here psalm [seventy-six], 'Aloud to God

how I cried', is properly added. It shows the road by which a man who by his own fault has strayed from God can return to happiness.

Psalm [seventy-seven], 'Harken, my people [to my teachings]' appropriately follows. It recalls the favors conferred by God on the Fathers of old. In like manner, it also treats of the punishments inflicted on those ungrateful for these favors. Man on the present pathway ought to strive to be mindful of both.

With the punishment of the ungrateful the next psalm [seventy-eight], 'O God, the nations have come [into your inheritance]', deals. Its theme is the desecration of the Temple and the dispersion of the jewish people. After the destruction of this people, a new people were given the light of faith; hence what follows.

In the second Nocturn, the first psalm [is psalm seventy-nine], 'O shepherd of Israel [hearken]'. Its theme is the coming of Christ by whom man is transformed from the old into the new.

Following next, psalm [eighty], 'Sing joyfully [to God, our strength]', has as its matter all who are baptized and justified by faith.

The next psalm [eighty-one], 'God stands in the divine assembly', speaks about the conversion of all the Jews to the faith so that from both [Gentiles and Jews] may be made one fold under one shepherd.* *Jn 10:16.*

At this point the psalmist turns to ponder the Last Things. There follows therefore psalm [eighty-two], 'O God, there is no one like you', which deals with the second coming of

Christ and the Last Judgment when the anti-
Christ and his followers will be sentenced to
eternal damnation.

Psalm [eighty-three], which follows, 'How
beautiful [is your dwelling place, O Lord of
hosts]', expresses a longing for a house of
God which is not man-made, but eternal in the
heavens. It is indeed a contemplative psalm.

After it comes psalm [eighty-four], 'You
have blessed [O Lord, your land]'. It has as
its subject matter the blessing bestowed on
mankind by Christ's first coming, which is
the primary cause of all subsequent benefits.

15. FRIDAY

The first psalm [is psalm eighty-five], 'Incline
[your ear, O Lord; answer me]'. It is the
prayer of a person given to meditation who,
mindful of his own insufficiency, recalls the
favors of God. And because prayer is generally
quickened by two considerations, the glory
to come and the graces of the present, psalm
[eighty-six], 'his foundation [is upon the
holy mountains]', is added. Dealing with
Jerusalem the heavenly city, it invites us
thereto. And psalm [eighty-eight], 'The mercies [of the Lord I will sing forever]', treats
the mercy and truth which Christ's coming
into the world brought in a great variety of
ways.

Psalm [ninety-two], 'The Lord reigns [in
splendor]', properly follows here. It discusses
the foundation of the earth, that is, the
Church, and the restoration of the human
race. It is followed by psalm [ninety-three],
'God of vengeance', which speaks of shining

lights, that is, saintly persons conspicuous for
their virtues and their heavenly manner of life.
It also alludes to those who blaspheme God, as
if accusing him of contempt of the world.

'Sing [to the Lord a new song; sing to the
Lord, all you lands]' [psalm ninety-five]
treats the building of the Church after the
coming of Christ.

After it [psalm ninety-six], 'The Lord is
king, [let the earth rejoice]' shows how
believers were transferred from the devil's
yoke to Christ's yoke after the Resurrection.

Psalm [ninety-seven], Sing to the Lord [a
new song, for he has done wondrous deeds]',
follows. It talks about the first coming of
Christ at the incarnation, and, in the latter
part of the psalm, about his second coming.

Next, psalm [ninety-eight], 'The Lord is
king, [the peoples tremble]', speaks of the
power of Christ reminding us that we must
adore Christ in the flesh as true God and true
man.

So it is that psalm [ninety-nine], 'Rejoice
[in the Lord, all the earth]', shows how we
must praise God at two levels. At best we
praise God for the benefits he has bestowed
on us; at least we accuse ourself of our
sins.

Yet because we do not reach this level
without purity of life, we add psalm [one-
hundred], 'Of kindness and judgment [I will
sing; to you, O Lord, will I sing praise]'. It
talks about the perfect justice which consists
in the choice of good things, above all of
mercy and justice. It also discusses the re-

jection of the wicked, detailed in the final
verses of the psalm.

16. SATURDAY

The first psalm [is one-hundred-one], 'O
Lord, hear my prayer'. It deals with the lowly
penitent who laments his own misery and the
wretchedness of the whole human race.

After this psalm of hope, there follows
psalm [one-hundred-two], 'Bless [the Lord,
O my soul]', which praises God for the favors
he has bestowed.

Using the same opening words, 'Bless [the
Lord, O my soul]' psalm one-hundred-three
not only praises God but also lists the works
for which we must praise Him.

A partial enumeration of these works,
among them the favors wrought by God for
the children of Israel is given in the following
psalm [one-hundred-four]: 'Give thanks to
the Lord; invoke his name'.

But because some of these children were
ungrateful for such great favors, psalm [one-
hundred-five], 'Give thanks to the Lord, [for
he is good]', is added next; it deals with the
rancorous bickering of the Jews.

This is followed by the third psalm which
has the same opening words, 'Give thanks to
the Lord [for he is good]' [psalm one-
hundred-six]. It reviews the four temptations
from which man is freed through the mercy
of God.

The psalm following [one-hundred-seven],
'My heart is steadfast, [O God, my heart is
steadfast]', is an exposition of this mercy. Its
theme is Christ himself acting in obedience

during his passion and in his glorification after his resurrection.

Then psalm [one-hundred-eight], 'O God of my praise, be not silent', describes more fully the sufferings of Christ; it deals not only with the passion of Christ but also denounces the traitor, Judas, and others who persecute Christ.

17. SUNDAY LAUDS

Having made brief comments on the psalms recited during Matins, I will now state the themes or subjects of the remaining psalms as the Hours succeed each other, making sure that simpler souls will easily understand them.

It is fitting that Lauds begin with psalm [sixty-six], 'May God have mercy on us and bless us', whose theme is the praise due God for the blessings he has bestowed on us through Christ after cancelling out the curse brought on by Adam. It is said after night— that is, the night of sin and unbelief*—has passed and the day—that is, the day of grace and enlightenment—has arrived.

Rm 13:12

Psalm [fifty], 'Have mercy on me, O God,' fittingly comes next. This psalm is about David doing penance in the name of all other sinners. It asserts that we must not despair on account of grievous sins but do penance. For we are obliged to praise God and give him thanks; and to admit and confess our sins.

This is followed by psalm [one-hundred-seventeen], 'Give thanks to the Lord [for he is good, for his mercy endures forever]'. Its only subject is Christ's mercy which he demonstrated by his first coming. The righteous person rejoices and is exceedingly glad in that day which God has made,* that is to say, the day of the Lord's resurrection, which gives us hope for our own resurrection.

Ps 117:24.

Building on this longing and hope, the following psalm [sixty-two], 'O God, you are my God', deals with the church set in the wilderness of Idumea,* that is, of this world. In exile from the Lord,* it longs to leave this life and be with Christ.*

2 Kgs 3:8.
2 Cor 5:6.
Ph 1:23.

Then follows the Song of Daniel* and the [three] psalms of praise† [148-150]. They praise God in both his rational and irrational creatures.

At the end is said the *Benedictus* canticle, 'Blessed be the Lord the God of Israel',* whose subject is the salvation of the world through the Saviour's Incarnation predicted in the birth of the Precursor.

Lk 1:68.

18. MONDAY LAUDS

The first psalm [five] is, 'Hearken to my words, O Lord'. Its theme is the inheritance of eternal life which follows this life's fleeting inheritance.

The next psalm [thirty-five], 'The unrighteous says [in his heart; there is no dread of God before his eyes]', lists the false teaching of some blasphemers who attribute all sins to our blemished and created [human] nature, and so overemphasize our free choice that they detract from divine grace.

The Canticle [of Isaiah 'On that day you will say, O Lord,] I give you thanks',* is

Is 12:1-16.

concerned with the coming of Christ.

19. TUESDAY LAUDS
The first psalm [is psalm forty-two], 'Judge
me, O God, [and fight my fight against a
faithless people]'. It speaks of the intermixture of grain with chaff, of weeds with
corn, that is, the intermixture of the good
with the bad in the Church Militant.

Then [follows psalm fifty-six], 'Have mercy on me, O God, have mercy' whose theme
is the passion and resurrection of Christ. The
last verses of the psalm clearly deal with his
glorious exaltation. The Canticle [of Heze-
kiah], 'I said, ["In the noontime of life I will
go to the gates of hell]"',* has as its subject
the onslaught of Hezekiah's illness and his
cure through God's grace.

Is 38:10-20.

20. WEDNESDAY LAUDS
Psalm [sixty-three], 'Hear, O God, my prayer
when I cry out', is the first psalm. In it Christ
speaks about harassments inflicted on himself
and on his followers. [Psalm sixty-four], 'To
you we owe a hymn of praise', deals with the
return from sin to penance, from harassment
to rest, from Babylon to Jerusalem.

The Canticle of Anna, 'My heart exults in
the Lord',* discusses the illumination of the
Church and the blindness of the synagogue.

1 Sam 2:1-10.

21. THURSDAY LAUDS
The first psalm [is psalm eighty-seven], 'O
Lord, God of my salvation'. Its theme is the
passion of Christ. [The following psalm,
eighty-nine,] 'O Lord, You have been our

Stephen of Sawley

refuge', is concerned with the old life and the new. The psalmist invites us to scorn the former and to love the latter.

The Canticle [of Moses], 'We will sing to *Ex 15:1-18.* the Lord [for he has triumphed gloriously,'* recalls the Israelites' passage through the Red Sea and the drowning of the Egyptians.

22. FRIDAY LAUDS

The first psalm [seventy-five], 'God is renowned in Judah, [in Israel great is his name]', deals with the Assyrians, that is, with directing our attention to God at all times.

And [the next psalm, ninety-one], 'It is good to give thanks to the Lord', is a psalm of instruction. Its theme is any good person who, when maligned, maintains a sabbath mind and, by comparison, the evil person who, when agitated has no sabbath.

The Canticle [of Habakkuk], 'O Lord, I *Hab 3:1-19.* have heard [your renown and been afraid]',* refers to the incarnation and passion of Christ.

23 SATURDAY AT LAUDS

The first psalm [is psalm one-hundred-forty-two], 'O Lord, hear my prayer'. It deals with the penitent who, by his example, invites others to penitence. The Canticle [of Moses], 'Give ear, O heavens, [while I *Deut 32:1-43.* speak]',* rebukes the Israelites who had crept back to the worship of idols.

24. SUNDAY AT PRIME

[The opening psalm, one-hundred-eighteen] 'Happy are they whose way is blameless, [who walk in the law of the Lord]' outlines the Law, that is, the teaching, of God. By the word 'Law' I mean the natural law, the Law of Moses in so far as it pertains to instruction, and the undefiled law of the gospel which refreshes souls. The psalmist shows what blessings God bestows on those who observe the law.

25. MONDAY AT PRIME

The theme of first psalm [psalm one], 'Happy the man [who follows not the counsel of the wicked]', is the whole Christ, the head and the members. At one time the psalm refers to Christ according to his godhead, at another according to his humanity and the restoration of mankind through the benefits of his incarnation. At the end the psalmist discusses the fate both of the good and of the reprobate. [Psalm two,] 'Why do the nations rage', speaks of Christ's kingship and the chastisement of those who reject him. [Psalm six,] 'O Lord, reprove me not in your anger', concludes that the penitent who humbles himself before God will be consoled by having his sins forgiven.

26. TUESDAY AT PRIME

The first psalm [is psalm seven], 'O Lord my God, in You have I hoped'. It deals with the mystery of man's redemption and the praise due God for that redemption. The theme of [psalm eight], 'O Lord, our Lord, [how glorious is your name over all the earth]', is Christ according to each nature. It also shows how the bad and the good co-exist in the church. [Psalm nine,] 'I will give thanks to You, [O Lord, with all my heart]', has as its subject matter the decisions of the Church for God in this life.

27. WEDNESDAY AT PRIME

The first psalm [psalm ten], 'In the Lord I put my trust', refers to the heretics who accept the sacred writings but have the effrontery to pervert their meaning. [Psalm eleven,] 'Save me, O Lord, [for no one now is dutiful]', shows how truth has been belittled and falsehoods multiplied in this world, and how this hinders those who are looking toward their heavenly rest,[1] that is, toward eternal happiness.

28. THURSDAY AT PRIME

[Psalm twelve,] 'How long, O Lord, [will you forget me?]', voices the longing of the faithful soul for Christ's coming and deplores the miseries of this exile. [Psalm thirteen,] 'The fool has said in his heart, [there is no God]', talks about those who scorn God and describes their maliciousness. [Psalm fourteen,] 'O Lord, who shall dwell in your tabernacle?]', describes those who are worthy of living in the heavenly Jerusalem; it makes a distinction between the worthy and unworthy.

29. FRIDAY AT PRIME

The first psalm [is psalm fifteen], 'Keep me, [O God, for in you I take refuge]'. Its subject matter is the kingdom of Christ, acquired through his sufferings. [Psalm sixteen,] 'Hear, O Lord, [a just suit, attend to my outcry]',

has as its theme Christ's prayer and shows
how we should pray when harassed. [Psalm
seventeen,] 'I will love You, [O Lord, my
strength]', recalls the freeing of Christ from
the power of his enemies, that is, the Jews
and Gentiles, death and the devil.

30. SATURDAY AT PRIME
The first psalm [is psalm eighteen], 'The
heavens declare the glory of God'. It refers to
the first coming of Christ which presaged the
preaching and miracles of the Apostles. [Psalm
nineteen,] 'The Lord hear you [in time of
distress]', considers the kingdom of Christ
and his priesthood.

31. THE VESPERS PSALMS
I will now list the subject matter of the
psalms at Vespers and of the nine psalms
which are said during the Little Hours of the
week as they follow in the psalmody, lest
their meaning be misconstrued by being
treated out of sequence.

The first Vespers psalm is [psalm one-
hundred-nine] 'The Lord said [to my Lord:
"Sit at my right hand"].' Its theme is Christ
according to each nature, but it treats the
human nature more extensively than the
divine. There follows [psalm one-hundred-
ten], 'I will give thanks [to the Lord, with all
my heart]' which praises God for having freed
his faithful people from eternal death and
having bestowed on them an everlasting inheritance. [Psalm one-hundred-eleven,]
'Blessed the man [who fears the Lord]', deals
with all the faithful who have been rescued

from the slavery of sin. [Psalm one-hundred-twelve,] 'Praise, you servants of the Lord, [praise the name of the Lord]', praises God for raising and dignifying human nature. [Psalm one-hundred-thirteen] 'When Israel came out of Egypt', has as its theme the one true God, and invites us to praise him. [Psalm one-hundred-fourteen,] 'I have loved [the Lord because he has heard my voice in supplication]', talks about the hundredth sheep which went astray in the wilderness* and the prodigal son,* that is, any believer who was first a drifter and sinner, but later on sincerely repented.

[Psalm one-hundred-fifteen,] 'I believed, even when I said', refers to the martyrs who publicly proclaimed their faith and imitated Christ's sufferings by giving witness to their faith. [Psalm one-hundred-sixteen,] 'Praise the Lord, [all you nations]', speaks of mercy inspired by faith, and truth crowned by merits.

[Psalm one-hundred-eighteen,] 'Happy are those whose way is blameless', has as its theme the Law of God, a teaching I have already explained.*

[Psalm one-hundred-nineteen,] 'In my distress I called to the Lord [and He answered me]': the first step is to long for the joys of heaven; this is meant by going up from Babylon to the heavenly Jerusalem. There were fifteen steps in Solomon's temple; the first seven symbolize the present life, the remaining eight the life to come. [Psalm one-hundred-twenty,] 'I lift up [my eyes toward the mountain whence shall come my help':

Mt 18:12.
Lk 15:11-32.

See above, Sunday at Prime.

the second step is diligent [self-] examination. [Psalm one-hundred-and-twenty one,] 'I rejoiced [when they said to me, "We will go up to the house of the Lord"]:' the third step is a mind full of joy as the light begins to glow within. [Psalm one-hundred-twenty-two,] 'To you, have I lifted up my eyes': the fourth step is obedience and devoted service. [Psalm one-hundred-twenty-three,] 'Had not the Lord been with us': the fifth step is the confession of one's own frailty.

[Psalm one-hundred-twenty-four,] 'They who trust in the Lord [are like Mount Zion]': the sixth step is trust in God's strength. [Psalm one-hundred-twenty-five,] 'When the Lord brought back the captives of Zion': the seventh step is unshakeable hope in eternal life. [Psalm one-hundred-twenty-six,] 'Unless the Lord [builds the house, they labor in vain who build it': the eighth step is the rejection of worldly honors in imitation of the Saviour. [Psalm one-hundred-twenty-seven,] 'Happy are all those [who fear the Lord]': the ninth step is a child-like fear of the Lord. [Psalm one-hundred-twenty-eight,] 'Often have they oppressed me from my youth': the tenth step is the acceptance of every kind of adversity. [Psalm one-hundred-twenty-nine,] 'Out of the depths I cry to you, O Lord': the eleventh step is the admission of all our wrongdoings. [Psalm one-hundred-thirty,] 'O Lord, my heart is not proud': the twelfth step is outward and inward humility. [Psalm one-hundred-thirty-one,] 'Remember, [O Lord, David and all his cares']: the thirteenth step is faith in the Lord's incarnation. [Psalm

one-hundred-thirty-two,] 'Behold how good
it is and how pleasant it is when brethren
dwell at unity': the fourteenth step is the
harmony which feeds brotherly love. [Psalm
one-hundred-thirty-three,] 'Come, now, [bless
the Lord, all you servants of the Lord]': the
fifteenth step is earnest thanksgiving, which is
but another word for loving God.

[Psalm one-hundred-thirty-four,] 'Praise
[the name of the Lord; praise, you servants of
the Lord]', praises God for the favors he
bestowed on our Fathers of old. [Psalm one-
hundred-thirty-five,] 'Give thanks to the Lord
[for he is good]', recalls the mercies of God
at the first creation and the benefits conferred later on. [Psalm one-hundred-thirty-
six,] 'By the streams of Babylon [we sat
down and wept]', treats of the inhabitants of
Jerusalem who were captives in Babylon.
Jerusalem is the city of the good, and Babylon
the city of the wicked. [Psalm one-hundred-
thirty-seven,] 'I will give thanks [to you, O
Lord, with all my heart]', shows how mercy
inspires faith and truth crowns merits. [Psalm
one-hundred-thirty-eight,] 'O Lord, you have
tested me', has as its theme Christ according
to both natures; however, psalmist treats his
human nature more fully than he does the
divine. [Psalm one-hundred-thirty-nine,] 'Deliver me, [O Lord, from evil men,]', talks
about how the church, exposed to both internal and external dangers, sighs and prays for
deliverance lest she follow the ways of the
wicked.

[Psalm one-hundred-forty,] 'O Lord, to
you I call', shows how Christ prays for his

own, and how the Church prays for herself
lest she yield to persecutors. [Psalm one-
hundred-forty-one,] 'With my voice [I cry out
to the Lord; with a loud voice I beseech the
Lord]', reveals how Christ prayed during the
time he was in the flesh. [Psalm one-hundred-
forty-three,] 'Blessed be the Lord, my rock',
talks about the church's victory over the
devil, defeated through the help of Christ.
[Psalm one-hundred-forty-four,] 'I will extol
you, [O God my king]' praises God who is
good to all and compassionate toward all his
works.*

Verse 9.

[Psalm one-hundred-forty-five,] 'Praise the
Lord, O my soul', is man's praise of God in
return for his salvation, a salvation which no
earthly prince can bestow. [Psalm one-
hundred-forty-six,] 'Praise the Lord [for he is
good]', has the same subject matter as its
immediate predecessor. [Psalm one-hundred-
forty-seven,] 'Praise the Lord, O Jerusalem',
praises God for having given peace and
security to the church.

32. COMPLINE

The first psalm [four] at Compline begins,
'When I call [answer me O God of justice]'.
It is a psalm of instruction concerned with
the true good of man so that at day's end,
when all senseless delights have been cast
aside, he may think about it. The following
[psalm ninety], 'You who dwell [in the
shelter of the Most High]', deals with temptations from the devil let loose openly or
secretly against man, which have been overcome by Christ or by his followers. Rightly

does this psalm follow the preceding, because all who wish to lead a holy life in Christ suffer persecution. But, as the last verses of the psalm make clear, they are freed from this persecution and from every tribulation.* So it is that [psalm one-hundred-thirty-three], 'Come now, [bless the Lord, all you servants of the Lord]',* properly follows next; its theme is fervent gratitude as a sign of our love of God.

Verses 14-16.

Ps 133.

A MEDITATION
on
THE LIFE AND PASSION OF CHRIST

33. NIGHT VIGILS

During the Night Office you should meditate, without straining the text of the psalms, on how Christ was born of the Virgin in the middle of the night and how the Light of the world lay hidden in darkness.*

Cf. Jn 1:5.

Behold him whom the whole world is not big enough to contain held within a crib; who, clothed with light as with a garment,* is wrapped in swaddling clothes;* who, crying in a crib casts his light all the way to heaven: who, pretending the weakness of an infant, rules all things by his divine power.

Ps 103:6.

Cf. Lk 2:7.

I know a man who thought thoughts like these while reciting psalm [eighty-eight], 'The mercies of the Lord [will I sing forever]'. By the time he reached the words, 'Yours are the heavens and yours is the earth', he was so caught up in the wonderment of unaccustomed sweetness that, hardly able to control himself, he addressed the Babe in the crib with a firm faith as if he were in his presence: 'Yours are the heavens and yours is the earth; you have founded the world and its fullness. Justice and judgment are the foundation of your throne; mercy and truth go before you. Happy is the people who know how to rejoice.' When he came to the next words and said, 'They walk in the light of your countenance, O Lord, and at your name they rejoice all day long . . . . ' you spoke once in a vision . . . , '* he felt almost drunk with joy, so overcome was he—so much so that even had he wished, he was not able, to express it.

Ps 88:12, 15, 16, 20.

I have given you this example because it is of recent origin, experienced while this was being written.

There are many passages in the psalms which are quite clear and thus well-suited for developing a sentiment of devotion and tender love.

During the Night Office we should think of the flight of his parents into Egypt: how Joseph took the child and his mother at night and retreated into Egypt; how his parents begged for themselves and for their child the fare of 'the poor on this journey. We read that until his twelfth year he was subject to his parents* and we believe that he, the God-Man, ministered to men in his humble home; that after being baptized by John, he did not abhor the solitude of the desert, but fasted and went hungry, he who is the bread of angels.*

Lk 2:41-51.

Ps 77:25.

He who by his word can restore to life all

those who are tempted and even those who
have lapsed, allowed himself to be tempted by
the devil. What labors he expended in preaching, travelling from place to place, tutoring
his disciples and teaching the people; how
Jn 4:6. tired he was when he sat down at the well*
Mt 8:20. and had no place of his own to lay his head.*
Think of the insults he suffered from the
Jews as they taunted him about his parents'
poverty, about dining with sinners, about
Mt 11:19. eating meat, about loving harlots.† Think
†Mt 21:31f. of how they dubbed him a winebibber, said
that he was possessed of devils and asserted
that he cast out devils through the prince of
Mt 12:24-28. devils.* Who can count all the verbal slurs
he suffered from them, all their efforts to
entrap him? First they sought to arrest him;
then they sent their henchmen, but his hour
had not yet come. First they wanted to throw
him over a mountain cliff cut he passed through
Lk 4:29. their midst and went his way;* then they
made ready to stone him, but he hid himself
from them. In all these instances, his wisdom
conquered their evil designs. In all these
instances the Son of God is giving us a lesson.
He does all these deeds in us. He has given us
lessons in humility, voluntary poverty, patience, and obedience until the end.

Have your meditation ponder no less the
effectiveness of the Son of God at prayer.
Consider, for instance, how at eventide Jesus
Mt 14:23. went up the mountain by himself to pray,*
Lk 6:12. how he spent the whole night in prayer*
earnestly beseeching his Father to save the
human race, and what solace and ministra-
Mt 4:11. tions he received from the angels;* how at the

night's third watch he came walking over the
water* to his disciples and saved them from
danger.   *Mt 14:25, Mk 6:48.*

To repress wandering of mind during the
Night Office, it will not be a fruitless exercise
for the young or the simple to think on these
and other like events in the life of Christ.

34. LAUDS

During Lauds, think of Jesus as he made his
way across the brook of Cedron to the garden
[of Gethsemani] where it was his custom to
pray. Consider how he took along Peter,
James, and John; how he then distanced
himself from them about a stone's throw;
how sad to the point of death and in anguish,
he prayed a long time; how his sweat fell like
drops of blood to the earth; how, on coming
back and discovering his three disciples asleep
he said to Peter, 'Simon, are you asleep?
Could you not watch one hour with me?'* If   *Mt 26, 27:1-10,*
you, too, are lazy, apathetic, or sleepy at that   *Mk 14, Lk 22,*
hour, say likewise to yourself: Simon, are   *Jn 18.*
you asleep? Obedient to Christ and aware of
his arrest and his prayer, so effective that it
brought about the shedding of his blood,
[ask:] Why are you so lukewarm? Could you
not watch with me one hour?

Consider Judas as he arrived with a squad
and betrayed his master with a kiss. Consider
Jesus as he gently returned his betrayer's kiss
and calmly asked, 'Friend, why have you
come?' Ponder how patiently he met the
mob which came armed with swords and
cudgels and offered himself up to suffer on
our behalf. Think of the henchmen as they

fell backwards and to the ground, and of his
disciples as they fled. Think of Jesus bound
and under arrest, being led before the tri-
bunal, slapped before Annas the high priest,
and gently answering 'If I have spoken evil,
[present evidence of that evil; but if I have
not, why do you strike me?],' by this giving
us an example of his extraordinary patience.

Finally, consider Peter as he followed from
afar and then cravenly denied his Master.
Consider Jesus as he looked mercifully at
Peter and Peter as he wept bitterly.

Think also how cruelly Jesus was dragged
from judge to judge, from Annas to Caiphas,
how without a word of human consolation he
Is 63:3.   trod the wine-press alone* and how of all
the human beings he created out of nothing
there was not one to console him. Peter denied
Mk 14:50-52.   him and John fled, leaving his robe behind.*
Thus Jesus stood alone before the high
priest; there he was accused by false wit-
nesses and condemned to death. He was spat
upon, struck and slapped, blindfolded and
all the while asked: 'Prophecy! Who hit you?'

But he surrendered his unblemished body
to those who struck him, and his cheeks to
Is 50:6.   those who plucked his beard.* He did not
turn away his face, that face on which angels
long to gaze, from those who reviled and spat
upon him. Let the high priests take fright, in
whose houses these things were done, where
Peter denied, and Jesus was flogged!

My dear friend, you must choose to be
flogged with Christ and remain in subjection
rather than deny him with Peter, by aspiring
to any position.

When you try out these suggestions, you should visualize—as I said a long while back—the circumstances of the actual events. For instance: stare at the rising sea, that is, at the carefully and maliciously conceived persecutions inflicted by faithless people on him who never did anything evil but instead did all things well for a people pecularly his own.*   *Deut 14:2.*

Admire then the Lord on high, who bore so kindly with Judas, who graciously healed the ear of his persecutor, who so mercifully looked on Peter and lifted him up after he had denied him. What love and affection he must have for his friends, when he shows so much toward his enemies!

But there is no need to list these themes for each and every Hour [of the Office]. As I have already said in connection with Lauds: to arouse your devotion during the other offices, picture in your mind these events and their circumstances.

35. PRIME

During Prime, think of Jesus condemned beforehand by the Jews who cruelly handed him over to Pilate, the gentile judge, imputing to him many false crimes.* But even the gentile Pilate, shocked at their villainy, answered them 'Take him yourselves and judge him in accordance with your own law'. But they, unwilling to be blameless in this criminal act, took advantage of the opportunity to charge him with having stirred up the people, beginning at Galilee. Hearing this, Pilate sent him to Herod, once the Jews had made their accusations, questioned him at

Mt 27:11-33; Mk 15:1-22; Lk 23: 1-25; Jn 18:28-40; 19:1-16.

length, treating this humble man with scorn. He had his soldiers mock him, had him dressed in a white robe and sent back to Pilate. This is how the Son of God was buffeted, dragged from judge to judge, stripped, and clothed again. In his own mockery, our Solomon took the part of a true peacemaker. From then on Herod and Pilate became friends.

Then Pilate, finding no justification for sentencing Jesus to death, promised that he would have him scourged; he did this not to make him suffer but rather to stay the savagery of the Jews. Pilate sought to free the innocent man, but they clamored all the more, 'Crucify, crucify him!' They were not satisfied with killing him just any way; they wanted to destroy him by a painful, dishonorable, and long-drawn-out death.

When Pilate countered, 'What evil has he done?', they shouted all the louder, 'Crucify him, crucify him'. They stood by their wicked cry. Realizing that he was accomplishing nothing, but that rioting was about to break out among the people, Pilate made a number of excuses, washed his hands, and pronounced the verdict that granted their demand.

Jesus was then handed over to the soldiers who stripped him of his clothes, cut his unblemished body with whips and cudgels, clothed him in a purple robe of derision, pressed a crown of thorns on his head, put a reed as a sceptre into his hands and, bending their knees, mocked him and said, 'Hail, King of the Jews'. They blindfolded him, hit him on the head with a reed, and said,

'Prophesy, Christ, who hit you?' This was how Pilate presented him to the people. In your meditation and imagination, ponder carefully how Jesus went out for your sake, not in the splendor of his power but covered with shame, wearing a crown of thorns and a purple robe.

And Pilate said to the Jews, 'Look at the man'. It is as if he were saying to them, 'Even if you envy the king, at least spare this scourged man whom you see in so abject a state. Let his blood, shed so barbarously and profusely, satisfy your thirst.' But they were to quiet down only after that innocent blood had flown fivefold.

Then he was led away by the soldiers to be crucified.

36. TERCE

At Terce, think of Jesus as he hurried to his place of execution, shouldering the cross laid on him with unheard-of cruelty.* Think also of the great crowd following him and of the weeping women, of how he lovingly turned to the women and said, 'Daughters of Jerusalem, do not weep over me [but for yourselves and your children]'. Think about how he arrived at long last at the place called Calvary,[2] that is to say, the place of the condemned; how, despising the shame,* he was raised on the Cross of his own free will, and how he hung between two thieves and was counted among the wicked.*

They brought to him a mixture of wine and vinegar,* which, when he had tasted it, he refused to drink. To those who offered him

*Mt 27:34-40; Mk 15:23-32; Lk 23: 26-38; Jn 19:17-22.

Heb 12:2.

Is 53:12.

*The roman soldier's wine ration.

vinegar he offered the sweetness of his intercession, saying, 'Father, forgive them, for
they do not know what they are doing'. Then
the soldiers divided up his garments, casting
lots for his [seamless] tunic.

Pilate wrote a victorious inscription, 'Jesus
of Nazareth, King of the Jews'. In his death
His kingship was corroborated thus. But his
enemies, the Jews, passing by, shook their
heads at him and said insultingly, 'Bah! You
were going to destroy God's Temple, why
don't you come down from that cross . . . ' .

37. SEXT

At Sext think of all the insults hurled at him,
of the darkness which enshrouded the earth
until the ninth hour. Think of these as evidence of the callousness of the Jews who were
insensitive to a grace so great that even
insensible and irrational creatures were aware
of it.*

*Mt 27:41-45,
Mk 15:33f.,
Lk 23:39-44,
Jn 19:23-30.

Consider the thieves, one on either side,
as one yelled blasphemies and reproaches at
him as if he were the worst of men, while the
other rebuked his companion and told the
Lord, 'Lord, remember me when you come
into your kingdom'. Just look at the faith of
that thief! And the Lord replied, 'Today, you
will be with me in paradise'. More marvelous
still is the mercy of the Saviour who, when he
came on behalf of sinners bestowed the first
fruits of his labors on a thief.

Then turn your attention to the Virgin
Mother and the disciple whom Jesus loved,
standing near the cross, looking at him with
tearful and loving eyes, feeling with him his

sufferings and sorrows, and suffering with
him as he suffered. For the sword of suffering
has pierced the mother's soul.*

Focus your mind on the loving Jesus as he
turned his compassionate eyes toward his
dear ones,* that is to say, as he entrusted his
mother to his disciple and the disciple to his
mother; in other words, as he entrusted
the Virgin to a virgin. This was his last testament on earth.

38. NONE

At None think of Jesus as he cried out in a
loud voice, 'My God, my God, why have you
forsaken me?,' mourning for us who have
been left behind. And when he said later on,
'I am thirsty', his thirst was not for this earth's
water, but for the salvation of mankind.*
They offered him cheap wine. But you, my
dear one, do not act like this; offer him
instead the wine of compunction and love.

At the very last, he said, 'It is finished'.
Completing his prayer, he added, 'Father,
into your hands I commend my spirit'. He
cried out with a loud voice, lowered His head
and gave up his spirit. What a truly sorrowful
sight! But the Saviour of the world has paid
death's debt and cancelled Adam's sin.

At this the veil of the Temple was torn
asunder, the earth quaked, rocks were split
apart, and tombs were opened as a sign of
the unlocking of the prison of hell and the
opening of the gates of heaven. At this many
bodies of those who slept were raised; they
came into the holy city and appeared to
many. When the centurion saw all this he

Lk 2:35.

**Mt 27:45-46,
Mk 15:34-41,
Lk 23:44-49,
Jn 19:31-37.*

said, 'Truly this was the Son of God'. If a
gentile centurion looking with physical eyes
felt this way, how ought the Christian given
to spiritual meditation be affected?

Finally, when the soldiers, anxious to break
his legs so the bodies could be taken down
more quickly, came to Jesus, they discovered
he was already dead. Thus, they did not break
a single of his bones,* but one of the soldiers
laid open his side with a lance and from it
blood and water gushed forth—a living fountain in which martyrdom, baptism, and the
Sacrament of the Altar have their origin.

Ps 38:21. Cf.
Ex 12:46.

This is how the Church was formed from
the side of Christ as he died on the Cross, just
as a woman was formed from the side of man
as he lay sleeping in paradise.

39. VESPERS

At Vespers think of how reverently Nicodemus
and Joseph lowered the body of Jesus from
the Cross, how carefully they wrapped the
body, preserved in spices, in a linen, how
faithfully the holy women and their friends
stood by, looking through their tears at the
lifeless limbs and at the places of the wounds,
and proceeded to wipe off the blood.*

Mt 27:57-66,
Mk 15:42-47,
Lk 23:50-56,
Jn 19:38-42.

How fortunate were all those who were
able to participate in this ministration, by
holding up his falling arms, by arranging his
splaying legs, by wiping up his blood as it fell
to the ground or by assisting in some way at
his burial, whether at the anointing, at the
wrapping of the body, or at its laying to rest.

40. COMPLINE

At Compline think of his gentleness. He let
himself be enclosed for our sake within the
narrowest of tombs, even though he is greater
than the heavens and broader than the sea,*   *Jb 11:9.*
and 'in his hands are the ends of the earth'.*   *Ps 94:4.*
Ponder how he on whom principalities, pow-
ers, and thousands of angels wait in heaven,
allowed himself to be guarded in his tomb by
a handful of soldiers.

Watch, therefore, and lie in wait as if you
were present at your Lord's grave so that you
can run immediately and support his steps as
he rises and leaves it. In your mind go with his
soul into hell and pay careful attention to the
awesome power with which he shattered the
gates of hell. Visualize the stupor which the
brilliant and unaccustomed light caused the
unclean spirits. Think of the great fear the
Lord put into them when he claimed their
powerful and well-armed prince and took his
tools away.* See what joy he flooded over the   *Cf. 2 Chr 20:25.*
over the elect who had been sitting in darkness
and in the shadow of death,* when he brought   *Lk 1:79.*
them light so they might see him and they
shouted and said, 'You have come, our Redeemer!' See how gloriously he led them forth
from that place of misery* and the jaws of the   *Ps 39:3.*
devil, all the way to his own wonderful light.*   *1 P 2:9.*

If you spend the canonical hours this way,
you will have a greater confidence in what
the Lord Jesus suffered for you during one
hour than you would have from your merits
or [personal] prayers. For, you must offer
back to God the Father his own works, not
furnish him with a heap of vanity derived

from your own efforts and actions. This is why it is good to be present at the Divine Office. Even if there are times when the mind wanders, the body is always occupied with such representations. And when the psalms are drawn out more slowly, the suffering of Christ becomes all the more evident in them. For then the cross of the Lord crucifies the monks who are standing suspended between two pieces of wood and, following Christ's example, crucified, because they can neither sit nor stir at their own volition but by the Order's regulations.

The wondrous efficacy of this sacred activity [the Divine Office] is far superior to all private prayer. For only 'he who combines the useful with the sweet', or, in our case, who applies the sweetness of such meditation to the contents of the psalms, 'will reap rewards in full measure'.*

*Horace, Ars Poetica, 343.

NOTES TO THE DIVINE OFFICE

1. *Octava,* meaning rest in heaven. Work on earth was a seven day affair, hence the eighth day was a day of rest, in heaven.
2. *Calvaria* (Latin), *Golgotha* (Aramaic), *Ras* (Arabic) = skull. Adam's head was supposedly buried there, hence 'the Skull'. Calvary was a piece of rocky ground north of Jerusalem. Probably the peculiar shape of the raised ground gave rise to the belief that it was the burial place of Adam's head.

TABLE OF ABBREVIATIONS

GENERAL ABBREVIATIONS

ABR	*American Benedictine Review,* Newark, Atchison 1950–.
ACW	Ancient Christian Writers series, Westminster (Maryland), Paramus (New Jersey), 1946–.
CCh	Corpus Christianorum series. Turnhout (Belgium), 1953–.
CF	Cistercian Fathers series. Spencer, Washington, Kalamazoo, 1970–.
Ep(p)	Epistola(e), Letter(s).
FCh	Fathers of the Church series. New York, 1948–.
Guignard	Philippe Guignard, *Les monuments primitifs de la règle cistercienne.* Dijon, 1878.
PL	J.-P. Migne, Patrologiae cursus completus, series Latina. Paris, 1844–66.
RAM	*Revue d'Ascétique et de mystique,* Toulouse, 1920–.
RB	*Regula monachorum / Rule of St Benedict.*
SBOp	*Sancti Bernardi Opera,* edd. Jean Leclercq, H.M. Rochais, C.H. Talbot. Rome: Editiones cistercienses, 1957–1982.
SCh	Sources chrétiennes. Paris: Editions du Cerf, 1941–.

THE WORKS OF AELRED OF RIEVAULX (c.1109–1166)

Ann	*Sermo in annunciatione* / Sermon for the Annunciation
Iesu	*De Iesu puero duodenni* / On Jesus at the Age of Twelve
Inst incl	*De institutione inclusarum* / Rule of Life for a Recluse

THE WORKS OF BALDWIN OF FORD (c.1140–1191)

Sacr	*De sacramento altaris* / On the Sacrament of the Altar

THE WORKS OF BERNARD OF CLAIRVAUX (1090–1153)

Adv	*Sermon in adventu domini* / Sermon for Advent
Asc	*Sermo in ascensione domini* / Sermon for Ascension
Asspt	*Sermon in assumptione beatae virginis Mariae* / Sermon for the Assumption
Circ	*Sermo in circumcisione domini* / Sermon for the Feast of the Circumcision
Csi	*De consideratione libri v* / Five Books on Consideration
Dil	*De diligendo Deo* / On Loving God
Epi	*Sermo in epiphania domini* / Sermon for Epiphany
JB	*Sermo in nativitate sancti Ioannis Baptistae* / Sermon for the Feast of the Nativity of St John the Baptist
Miss	*Homilia super* missus est *in laudibus virginis matris* / Homilies in Praise of the Virgin Mother
Nat BVM	*Sermo in nativitate beatae virginis Mariae* / Sermons for the Nativity of Our Lady
O Asspt	*Sermo dominica infra octavam assumptionis* / Sermon for Sunday within the Octave of the Assumption
O Epi	*Sermo in octava epiphania domini* / Sermon within the Octave of Epiphany
p Epi	*Sermo in dominica I post octavam Epiphaniae* / Sermon for the First Sunday after the Octave of Epiphany
Pent	*Sermo in die sancto pentecostes* / Sermon for Pentecost Sunday
Pur	*Sermo in purificatione beatae virginis Mariae* / Sermon for Candlemas
SC	*Sermo super Cantica canticorum* / Sermon on the Song of Songs
V Nat	*Sermo in vigilia nativitatis domini* / Sermon for Christmas Eve

THE WORKS OF GILBERT OF HOYLAND (†1172)

SC   *Sermo in Cantica canticorum* / Sermon on the Song of Songs

THE WORKS OF GUERRIC OF IGNY (1070?–1157)

Asspt   *Sermo in assumptione beatae virginis Mariae* / Sermon for the Assumption

THE WORKS OF ISAAC OF STELLA (1100?–1167?)

1 Epi   *Sermo septimus, in dominica post Epiphaniam* / Sermon Seven: For the Sunday after Epiphany

O Epi   *Sermo nonus, in dominica I post octavam Epiphaniae* / Sermon Nine: For the First Sunday after the Octave of Epiphany

THE WORKS OF WILLIAM OF ST THIERRY (†1148)

Cant   *Expositio super Cantica canticorum* / Exposition on the Song of Songs

Contemp   *De contemplando deo* / On Contemplating God

Ep aur   *Epistola [aurea] ad fratres de Monte-Dei* / The Golden Epistle to the Brethren of Mont-Dieu

Psalms have been cited according to the Vulgate enumeration, as Stephen of Sawley cited them. All other scriptural passages have been cited according to the enumeration and nomenclature of *The Jerusalem Bible*.

A BIBLIOGRAPHY OF WORKS CITED

Adam de Perseigne. *Lettres I*. Ed. Jean Bouvet. Sources chrétiennes, 66. Textes monastiques, 4. Paris, 1960.

Adam of Perseigne. *The Letters of Adam of Perseigne*. Trans. Grace Perigo. Cistercian Fathers Series, 21. Kalamazoo, 1976.

Aelred de Rievaulx. *La vie de recluse*. Ed. Charles Dumont. Sources chrétiennes, 76. Textes monastiques, 2. Paris, 1961.

Aelred of Rievaulx. *Rule of Life for a Recluse*. Trans. Mary Paul Macpherson. *Aelred of Rievaulx. Treatises One*. Cistercian Fathers Series, 2. Spencer, 1971.

Aelred de Rievaulx. *Quand Jesus eut douze ans*. Ed. Anselme Hoste. Sources chrétiennes, 60. Textes monastiques, 1. Paris, 1958.

Aelred of Rievaulx. *On Jesus at the Age of Twelve*. Trans. Theodore Berkeley. *Aelred of Rievaulx. Treatises One*. Cistercian Fathers Series, 2. Spencer, 1971.

Amadeus de Lausanne. *Huit homélies*. Edd. Jean Deshusses and A. Dumas. Sources chrétiennes, 72. Textes monastiques, 5. Paris, 1960.

Amadeus of Lausanne. *Homilies*. Trans. Grace Perigo. *Magnificat. Homilies in Praise of the Blessed Virgin Mary*. Cistercian Fathers Series, 18, Kalamazoo, 1979.

Augustine of Hippo. *Christian Instruction*. Trans. John J. Gavigan. Fathers of the Church, 4. New York, 1947.

——————————— *The Confessions of St Augustine*. Trans. Vernon J. Bourke. Fathers of the Church, 21. New York, 1953.

——————————— *Sermons on the Nativity*. Trans. M. Muldowney. *Sermons on the Liturgical Year*. Fathers of the Church, 38. New York, 1959.

——————————— *The Trinity*. Trans. Stephen McKenna. Fathers of the Church, 45. New York, 1963.

Baudouin de Ford. *Le sacrament de l'Autel*. Edd. Jean Leclercq, John Morson, E. de Solms. Sources chrétiennes, 93-94. Textes monastiques, 12-13. Paris. 1963.

Cyprian of Carthage. *Mortality (De mortalitate)*. Trans. R. J. Deferrari.

Cyprian of Carthage. Treatises. Fathers of the Church, 36. New York, 1958.

Gilbert of Hoyland. *Sermons on the Song of Songs 1–3.* Trans. Lawrence C. Braceland. Cistercian Fathers Series, 14, 20, 26. Kalamazoo, 1978, 1979, 1979.

Guillaume—See William.

Hallier, Amédée. *The Monastic Theology of Aelred of Rievaulx.* Cistercian Studies Series, 2. Spencer, 1969.

Hymn Book of the Martyrs. Trans. M. Clement Eagan. Fathers of the Church, 43. New York, 1962.

Isaac de l'Étoile. *Sermons.* Ed. Anselme Hoste and G. Galet. Sources chrétiennes, 130. Textes monastiques, 20. Paris, 1967.

Isaac of Stella. *Sermons on the Christian Year,* 1. Trans. Hugh McCaffery. Cistercian Fathers Series, 11. Kalamazoo, 1979.

James, Bruno Scott, trans. *The Letters of St Bernard of Clairvaux.* Chicago, 1953.

John Cassian. *Jean Cassien. Conférences.* Ed. J.-C. Guy. Sources chrétiennes, 42, 54, 64. Paris, 1955-1959.

John of Damascus. *The Orthodox Faith. John of Damascus. Writings.* Trans. Frederic H. Chase, Jr. Fathers of the Church, 37. New York, 1958.

Origen. *Exhortation to Martyrdom.* Trans. John J. O'Meara. Ancient Christian Writers, 19. Westminster, 1956.

Sulpicius Severus. *Letter of Sulpicius Severus to the Deacon Aurelius.* Trans. Bernard M. Peebles. Fathers of the Church, 7. New York, 1949.

William of St Thierry. *Guillaume de Saint Thierry. La Contemplation de Dieu. L'oraison de Dom Guillaume.* Ed. Jacques Hourlier. Sources chrétiennes, 61 bis. Textes monastiques, 2. Paris, 1968.

William of St Thierry. *On Contemplating God.* Trans. Penelope Lawson. *On Contemplating God. Prayer. Meditations.* Cistercian Fathers Series, 3. Spencer, 1970.

Guillaume de Saint-Thierry. *Exposé sur le Cantique de cantiques.* Ed. Jean-Marie Déchanet. Sources chrétiennes, 82. Textes monastiques, 8, Paris, 1962.

William of St Thierry. *Exposition on the Song of Songs.* Trans. M. Columba Hart. Cistercian Fathers Series, 6. Spencer, 1970.

Guillaume de Saint-Thierry. *Lettre aux Frères du Mont-Dieu.* Ed. Jean-Marie Déchanet. Sources chrétiennes, 223. Textes monastiques, 14. Paris, 1975.

William of St Thierry. *The Golden Epistle of William of St Thierry.* Trans. Theodore Berkeley. Cistercian Fathers Series, 12. Spencer, 1971.

INDEX OF PATRISTIC AND MEDIEVAL AUTHORS
CITED OR REFERRED TO IN NOTES

Aelred of Rievaulx
  Ann
    96
  Iesu
    43, 44, 96
  Inst Incl
    61, 96, 106, 107, 109,
    114, 121, 122
  Spec car
    93

Alcuin of York
  69

Amadeus of Lausanne
  Homilies
    28, 29, 31, 33, 37, 50,
    51, 53, 54, 56, 57, 61,
    96

Augustine of Hippo
  Confessions
    66, 67, 69, 145
  The City of God
    73
  Enchiridion
    98
  Enarrationes in psalmos
    107
  Sermons on the Nativity
    33, 41, 61
  Sermons for Epiphany
    40
  The Trinity
    55, 68, 73, 81

Baldwin of Ford
  Sacr
    99, 101

Bernard of Clairvaux
  Adv
    70
  Asc
    52
  Asspt
    31, 57
  Circ
    39
  Csi
    72, 73
  Dil
    69, 128, 145
  Epi
    39, 40
  Ep(p)
    70
  JB
    46, 62
  Miss
    31, 32, 61, 96
  Nat BVM
    29, 30
  O Asspt
    27, 34, 48, 71
  O Epi
    45
  Pent
    33, 34
  p Epi
    31
  Pur
    41, 62
  SC
    39, 45, 106, 107, 136,
    145
  V Nat
    47
  = Ernaldus
    69

INDEX OF SCRIPTURAL CITATIONS AND ALLUSIONS

TITLES LISTING

THE CISTERCIAN FATHERS SERIES

THE CISTERCIAN STUDIES SERIES

* *Temporarily out of print*   † *Forthcoming*

THOMAS MERTON

THE CISTERCIAN LITURGICAL DOCUMENTS SERIES †

FAIRACRES PRESS, OXFORD

Distributed in North America only for Fairacres Press.

DISTRIBUTED BOOKS

* *Temporarily out of print*   † *Forthcoming*